"Negative thoughts so easily seep into our minds. And unknowingly, they determine our future. We go through each day on autopilot. Many times wondering why things just don't go our way. Chris taught me the power of shredding negative thoughts. By taking control of my thoughts and mentally shredding the negative ones, I put my life on a MUCH more positive path! I stopped creating drama in my relationship with my spouse, became more understanding in my relationships with others and landed a dream job. Control of our thoughts enables us to reach our full potential."

KATIE BIELKE
EXECUTIVE ASSISTANT

"Chris is very well versed in Servant Leadership and is very articulate in getting his message across. I have also read Chris' book, ThoughtShredder, and applied his process in overcoming my personal challenges. I believe everyone can benefit from the ThoughtShredder principles and become more successful both personally and professionally."

KEVIN LEURQUIN
PRESIDENT AT LIFE IS A SWING, FOLLOW THROUGH

"When you need to be at the top of your game, or to be at your best, you cannot have any negative thoughts in your head. Chris' ThoughtShredder process is the way to get rid of those negative thoughts, so you can be your best!"

NORB WEST
FINANCIAL SERVICES PROFESSIONAL

"The ThoughtShredder tool is quick and easy to use. It can be used any time to clear the clouds of negative thinking and allow us to see the sunshine that each day brings!"

KEVIN NASAL
RN

THOUGHT
SHREDDER

BRINGING OUT THE BUCKER IN YOU

CHRIS ELLIOTT

9th
street
publishing

154 N. Broadway
Green Bay, WI 54303

THOUGHTSHREDDER:
BRINGING OUT THE BUCKER IN YOU

For more information and copies of
this book, please visit:
www.9thstreetpublishing.com

Published by:
9th Street Publishing
154 N. Broadway, Green Bay, WI 54303

Cover Design and Layout by: Prophit Marketing
www.prophitmarketing.com

Manufactured in the United States of America

THOUGHT
SHREDDER

TABLE OF CONTENTS

ACKNOWLEDGEMENTS

To my wife Tracy and my five children, thank you for believing in me through all of my failures and allowing me to learn to be a better husband and father.

To my mother Bernadine, thanks for being the first Bucker I ever knew and teaching me that we all can make choices to create a new life at any time.

To my father Dallas, I now know that I love you and miss you. You did the best you could with what you knew.

THOUGHT
SHREDDER

BRINGING OUT THE BUCKER IN YOU

INTRODUCTION

Did you ever question who you are, what you are doing, or why you are here on this earth? These are very common introspective questions we all ask at some point. Like most people I have met, there were times when I wondered who I really was and what my true purpose was. These were obvious questions and I asked them frequently. These were logical questions I was seeking logical answers for. There were other questions lingering. Questions I could not quite ask. They were on the tip of my tongue, but I couldn't get them out. These were the difficult questions, the ones that would really change my life if only I knew how to ask them.

Over time, I would be able to ask these questions and work to uncover the answers. Both haunted me for many years—from about age five until I was forty-one years old. They began to be revealed to me in June, 2006. However, I'm still not totally comfortable with my answers. I guess it is different for everyone as much as we like to throw blanket responses over all situations.

On that day in June, I was standing in my kitchen with my wife when we got the news. It came from my mother as we hit the play button on our home answering machine, "There's no other way to say this except, your father died yesterday morning." As I stood in that kitchen holding my wife in my arms, I struggled to cry. My father just died, shouldn't I be sad? Instead, I was numb. In that moment, I realized that losing my dad started some thirty-six years earlier. I was forty-one years old and my dad was gone; I was five years old when I began to lose him.

Between the ages of five and forty-one, as with all of us, so many changes occurred in my life. I grew up physically during those years, but didn't really mature. I was provided hundreds, even thousands of lessons, but wasn't ready to hear all of them. I graduated college, started my career, married a wonderful lady and we started our family together. I seemingly had everything I could want, but I still wondered what was missing. Then the questions began to come.

When a father holds his newborn baby and cares and nurtures that baby for the first few months of his life, is an unbreakable bond created? If so, how long does it take to form? If that bond is breakable, where is the line that determines the breaking point? If the breaking point is reached, what does the child do from there? These were questions my heart was asking. They were on the tip of my tongue for so many years because my heart needed to know, but parts of my heart had been so buried that I could not reach them. I had to become a Bucker before I could reach them.

A Bucker is someone who looks at their childhood experiences and defiantly says, "No, I do not have to live that life!" They look at statistics that show a high percentage of children who grow up in alcoholic families will become alcoholics and they say, "Watch me not become one." Similarly, Buckers who grow up in abusive families say, "Not me! I will show you that I can be the opposite!" They are the ones who defy others when they say, "You can't do that." The Bucker response: "Oh yeah? Just watch me." And the Bucker does it.

That was me for a good part of my life. I often bucked the trivial things and occasionally the big things. The most important bucking took real effort and the breaking and rebuilding of a bond.

Becoming a Bucker required that I find the bond that existed between my father and myself, and then break it. It required that I identify circumstances that I no longer wanted to be part of. It started with subtle unconscious choices, moved to conscious choices and remains a journey that lasts a lifetime. On the way, I lost parts of my heart, burying them under layers of garbage, trying to protect myself from becoming the person I feared most. I had to find a process to help me rediscover my heart, unbury it and become the person I wanted to be.

Like anyone else, a Bucker's childhood determines much of what his nature, traits, personality, quirks and lifestyle will be like. Those early childhood events shape how we will view life. It starts with the bond between a parent and a child and proceeds with the interactions between the parent and the child. Most children want to grow up to be their dad, to live the honorable life he led. Being a Bucker against your dad means wanting to live any other way.

For too long, I was looking for the logical answer. What I grew to discover later in life, however, was that my heart had to define it too. My heart knew all along, but it took several Bucker moments along my journey to see and feel the answers. It took an opening of my heart and an acceptance of God's greatest gift to get the answers. It took forgiveness. That forgiveness helped me rebuild a bond I had worked so hard to break.

Forgiveness wasn't easy and it didn't come naturally. I discovered it through a process called "ThoughtShredder" that allowed me to begin tearing away at the bond my father and I had, along with all the negative beliefs I had about myself. The process has four simple steps: Recognize, Rid, Replace and Reinforce. By utilizing this process over and over again, I was able to break apart from my father emotionally, see him as a different person, and begin to understand him. Once I understood him, I could reconnect with him and forgive. Only then could I begin to be successful for myself.

This book explains my journey and the process I used. It is split into two main sections. If you are someone who likes a story, read the whole book from beginning to end. You'll get my story and how to use the ThoughtShredder process. If you prefer to go right to the process, you can start at the end of the book at Chapter 14 and read how the process works.

I won't tell you that my life is perfect, but it is much further on that path than it has ever been before. I hope you enjoy my story.

1

MEMORIES BEGIN

The view from our sunroom to the backyard play area is a wonderful sight during this afternoon as I watch my children play. Lauren is swinging on a swing, tipping her body as far back as she can so that her feet are well above her head. Her long brown hair brushes the sand below the swing as she moves forward. She pulls herself upright again as the swing moves back.

She's her mother: long and lean with a daintiness that is very charming. For a girl going into second grade, she seems a bit frail to me when she's really just growing into her frame. She is what we call peace/fun in behavioral terms. This makes her quite lovable by most, while very sensitive to the needs of others. She's likely to break many hearts when she gets older, as well as having her own broken many times. Her quiet resolve won't allow her to share her broken heart with anyone who isn't very close to her.

The sky is bluer than seems fair while a light breeze brushes the tree branches aside allowing the scent of freshly mowed grass to drift over the backyard fence and into the house. As wonderful as the weather is, the splendor of the day has little to do with that. Today is just another step in my journey and I'm learning to enjoy each step.

Lauren repeats a teeter-totter motion with her body on the swing over and over as I watch. A year ago, I would have leaned out the patio door and shouted her name, letting her know that Dad didn't approve of her reckless swinging.

"But why, Dad?" she would question.

"Because it's too dangerous and you look like you're going to fall off the swing," would be my reasoning response. It's my job to keep her safe. She's a good girl and would immediately stop, but wish that she didn't have to.

Today I let her swing her way, trusting that she's skilled enough to keep herself safe. Things are different for me now that I understand the Bucker in me. My decisions are less conservative these days. I think more about my children's freedom and growth and less about my needs. I have much more faith in their ability to learn and sense right from wrong, danger from safety. I give them much more rein to explore and grow their independence from me.

Carson and Megan are running around the backyard. They disappear through the back door of the garage, and then pop back out into the backyard again. Carson is behind Megan just on her heels, but being only five, he can't quite catch up to his seven-year-old sister. I'm poised with an open mouth, about to tell to Megan how she needs to understand that her brother is only five and she should let him catch her once in a while. But I stop myself and just watch. My open mouth closes and forms a smile instead. He'll catch her one day, in his own time.

The rustling sounds of a five-month-old bring my attention to the living room just a few feet from the sunroom. Aiden, the older twin boy is just waking up. Soon his rustling sounds will turn into cries as he lets me know of his need for a bottle. I anticipate his need and hasten myself into the kitchen.

Pulling the bottles out of the cupboard, my attention is again broken by the cry of Owen. The other twin is awake and will need a bottle too. "Way to go Aiden, your crying woke up your brother and now both of you need to be fed," I say to myself in pretend disgust.

Just before the bottles can be made, Lauren opens the patio door and shouts her request for a juice box. I grant her permission and direct her to the refrigerator in the garage. The twins are crying harder now that they see me walking toward them with a bottle in each hand. Just as I reach them and begin the effort of staging them on my lap in a way that allows me to feed a bottle to both at the same time, Carson comes in crying.

"What happened?" I force out, not really looking forward to what I expect will be a drawn out, one-sided answer.

"Megan tripped me," he replies as he peeks through his hands that are cupping his face. His pleading look is broken by a grin he can no longer hold back. That grin helps me realize that he's not really hurt and his tears are part of him staging drama.

"Tell Megan to come in here," is my dutiful response as Dad.

I'm now situated correctly on the couch and feeding the twins as Megan comes in and starts to immediately explain how Carson pushed her first. On the explanations go, back and forth between the two, each ending with blame towards the other.

I end the see-saw with a quick question, "Megan, did you trip Carson on purpose?"

"Yes," she forces out in a low tone hardly moving her lips.

"Then what do you say?"

"Sorry, Carson."

"It's okay," comes his now cheery response as they hug. Then they're off to the backyard ready to play again and likely interrupt me in a few minutes with another "crisis".

This is the way I'm teaching my children to show forgiveness. If you're at fault, say you're sorry; intentional or accidental, you always say you're sorry. The recipient child feels better, forgives you and silently asks that you never do that again. Forgiveness is a wonderful event to witness, but I've learned its effects are even greater when you are the one forgiving. It is a lesson that took me on a journey of recounting my past and bringing it in touch with my present.

These are the days I live now. It appears I will be living them for some time. Hectic, frustrating, rewarding, and I love every moment even if I don't realize it at the time. These are the images of a seemingly normal family life. As others watch us and share time with us, do they see normalcy or do they see what's hidden underneath? Do they know the struggle it took to get here and the struggle to keep us on this path?

Still feeding the twins, I start to think back about my childhood. These days, it's rare that I don't pause to reflect when an event happens in my family and wonder how I would have felt about it as a kid. What were my parents feeling at this time in their lives? I remember much of what they did, how they acted, but I wonder what they were actually thinking and feeling. Did they doubt themselves ever? Did they have dreams for a better life?

The twins fall asleep while I feed them, but Owen quickly wakes and can't get comfortable. I pick him up gently and snuggle him to my chest, rubbing his back. He turns his head away, closes his eyes and goes back to sleep. It's hard to tell if my gentle strokes on the soft warmth of his little head are caressing him or if it is my hand being caressed. Is it for his benefit or mine? While it puts him to sleep, it puts me in awe. I wonder if my dad ever had that same thought.

"I love you," I whisper to him with a gentle kiss. We rock on the chair together for a short time and the memory of my dad holding Julie in his arms flashes in front of me. It's a black and white picture of my sister that I remember. The picture shows Dad wearing a white t-shirt and dark pants holding Julie while seated on the couch. I wasn't yet born when the picture was taken, but I've seen it in one of Mom's picture albums many times. I look down now and notice I too am wearing a white t-shirt. For a moment that familiar, tormenting question repeats in my head, "How much am I like Dad?" Memories begin to cascade.

"Hey, Scott, watch this!" I shout across the bridge as I try to slide my five-year-old body down the large cement column at the end of the bridge. Each end of each side of the bridge brings the metal railings of the main bridge down to the ground with these cement angles.

The railings are metal guards meant to protect us from falling through the bridge and into the water. There are three sets of them running the length of the bridge on each side, painted a steel blue with many spots of rust beginning to show. They do an adequate job of protecting us, but if we really wanted, we could get through. If we did, we'd fall some fifteen feet into the muddy water below.

The cement columns are easily wide enough to hold my body. They jab straight out from the ends of the bridge for about two feet, and then angle down another four feet or so until each end drops off sharply to the ground. They are meant to stabilize some part of the bridge, I imagine. Today, they are my slides.

The sudden drop off of the cement column forces me to jump a bit at the end in order to accurately hit the ground on my feet. The slide doesn't work very well, I discover. The cement is too rough to allow me to slide. Instead, I have to squat with my butt just off the cement, my hands beneath my shoulders and my sunk-in stomach facing the sky as I walk on my hands and feet down the angle. It was a good thought, and fun anyway. I'm five, so I jump back on it to try again. It will take a few more attempts before I get it.

This is my first memory of seeing the bridge. I'm certain I had been there before, but I can't recall any of the specifics from earlier times.

The bridge spans the Manitowoc River for about sixty feet. The river is huge in my eyes, but in reality is only about forty feet wide at this spot and goes from five or six feet deep in the spring to about two feet deep by mid-summer. By then, the weeds are growing through much of it and rocks begin to poke through the surface. We don't mind. Fishing is still fun no matter how low the water is.

The view through a five-year-old's eyes sees a wondrous, powerful river that has to be the largest waterway in the world. And, really, it was. It was the largest in *my* world. This must have been what Tom Sawyer and Huck Finn thought of the great Mississippi when they first saw it, but this is no Mississippi. It's just one of thousands of small rivers in the state, but this one is a quarter mile behind my house and we live closer to it than anyone else. It's *our* bridge and this part of the river is *our* river. That's the way Dad made it feel.

We'd go down to the bridge on summer weekends with five-gallon pails and a fishing rod in each kid's hand. We'd meet my uncle down there, and some cousins, and fish until all the buckets were full of bullheads. On a rare occasion, Dad would accidentally snag a northern. I didn't know what that meant, but everyone would scream with excitement when it jumped out of the water. Suddenly, all other rods were neglected as we all gathered around Dad watching him battle this beast of a fish. He'd pull in this skinny, long fish with silver on its sides. It was certainly longer than a bullhead, but much skinnier. Dad would take it off the line, show it to everyone, and then throw it back in the water. I wasn't impressed. We could eat the bullheads; that impressed me.

My brothers and I fished at that bridge many, many times until I was about twelve. Then Dad left and I didn't really feel like fishing anymore. I've fished only a time or two since. How many other changes have I allowed since Dad left?

Other weekend days or nights were spent with some moments of Dad, generally wearing that white t-shirt, wrestling with us on the front lawn or the living room carpet. My three brothers and I would be out on the front lawn as the sun began to lower in the sky bringing cooler temperatures back to what was a sweltering day. Supper is done and cleaned up. It's time to play some football—which usually means Dallas and I against Scott and Jeff.

It's a normal summer day at the Elliott household. Our family consists of five children including four boys and one girl, she being the oldest. I'm the youngest and seven years separate me from my older sister. It all seems common to me. Doesn't everyone have five children and play football and basketball in the front yard during the summer? Doesn't everyone have a mother and father who care for them and protect them? Aren't we the normal family?

That's the façade I will build and portray for most of my life; hiding the reality even from myself at times.

CHAPTER LESSONS

Abuse exists within homes and families that are seemingly normal. We see those families every day, but we don't realize what they are hiding.

Buckers exist in these families who are seemingly normal. They might be covering up initially, but they will fight to become different than what they see inside their home.

Don't be fooled by the seemingly perfect scenes of other families. We all have issues at some level. How much do we cover up?

ThoughtShredder Moment

These experiences as a child create what I call the "blackboard" of our lives. Our influences are etched into the blackboard and continue to build upon each other. These are the set of circumstances, events and relationships that form who we are as adults. The blackboard begins to form the basis of who we are. It will control us in our adult lives.

I refer to this as a blackboard because, like a teacher's blackboard, we often assume that what is written there is accepted as accurate, true and fact. It is not up for debate. We don't even realize this is happening. It reminds me of the concept of electricity. I don't know how it works or why it works, but I use it every day. I take it for granted each day when I flip on the light switch that electricity is powering my ability to eliminate the darkness. How and why this blackboard runs my life is not important. That it does is very important.

The Bucker understands the concept of the blackboard. Others call it programming, nature, upbringing, or hard-wiring. Certainly some of our adult events help shape us also, but the foundational elements that are buried deep in our brains are the things that drive us most. They set up the foundation of beliefs and values that we allow to run our lives. We carry that blackboard with us our entire lives.

For some, the blackboard is perfectly written on. Their childhood experiences were with parents who were firm, but fair, treated them as unique individuals and celebrated successes. Some grew up in a loving, nurturing family without abuse or neglect. Many of us grew up in homes full of chaos and appear destined to live chaotic adult lives as well.

Many of us, without realizing it, believe we cannot change it. This is when you hear phrases like, "That's the way I was raised," or "I got that from my dad." True statements, unfortunately, they are too often followed by, "I can't help it." That's where they are wrong.

A Bucker is one who uses a process to counteract the blackboard. A Bucker chooses to defy the blackboard and rewrite it for himself. Thought-Shredder is the process for me and it starts by understanding your own blackboard.

ACTION PLAN

Start your ThoughtShredder journey with some pre-work. Take some time to think about the events of your childhood. Start with the happy times and grow into the chaos. Write as much of it down as you can to really get the scenes flowing. Soon you will start to uncover scenes you thought you had totally forgotten. If other family members are available, ask them about certain childhood times. Soon the scenes will begin flowing like mini-movies in your brain. This is the start of your new life.

My Journey

2

INNOCENT BEGINNING

The twins are sleeping now and the warmth of the sun is calling me outside. The warmth–and Carson's voice–are calling me.

"Dad, Dad!" come the yells from Carson's soft voice. It's a pleading call that I can distinguish from his previous calls for help. I'm confident he wants to do something. I begin tying my tennies in anticipation.

"Dad, are the babies sleeping yet? You promised to play outside when they went to sleep."

"They just went down," I reply as I spring off the couch to chase him out the sunroom door to the backyard. He screams with laughter and runs as fast has he can run, back out the door and onto the grass. He picks up a football from the grass as he runs, stumbles and falls to ground. I catch up to him lying on the ground and I dive over him yelling, "Fumble!"

He's laughing uncontrollably as we wrestle for the pretend fumble. It seems to be the best time he's ever had in his life. I let him wrestle the ball from me and run to the end of the lawn for a touchdown. He wins.

"Try to get it from me again," Carson says in a now teasing voice.

I run after him, catch him and playfully tackle him knocking the football out of his hands. We wrestle some more. I am instinctively cautious not to roll over him, or catch his little arm or leg in an awkward position. At only five feet seven inches, I'm a small man, but a giant in his eyes. With more than a hundred-pound advantage on him, I could easily hurt him and ruin the fun we're having together. I don't have to think about this; it just comes naturally to me. It's part of my Bucker programming.

"That's not fair!" Carson screams as I continue to tap the ball just out of his reach. It was fun at first, but now he's tired of not getting the ball, so I let him reach it. The words he uses ring in my ears. I hear them over and over for a few seconds, but the voice is not Carson's; it's mine …

"That's not fair!" come the screams of a five-year-old, tears mixed with sweat on my face. The tantrum is about to start with me continuing to scream in defense of my position that Scott cheated. Scott is ready to defend his actions saying I wasn't down. Back and forth we'll go arguing our points until Dallas jumps in to snap the next play. Then it's my turn to get even by beating Scott deep for a long touchdown. That's the intended scene, but this one gets halted before the next play can start.

It's front lawn football at the Elliott's house. Dallas and Jeff are all-time quarterbacks because I can't throw the ball far enough or accurately enough for Dallas to play wide receiver. Scott gets to cover me as I go out for the first pass. Dallas steps back and hits me right on target. It's a short route making it easier for me to make the catch. I'd like to think I've run a good route creating space for Dallas to throw the ball, but in reality, Scott lets me get open. He does it so he can catch me, hold me up and rip the ball out of my arms. I try to force myself down to the ground to end the play, but Scott is a year and a half older, bigger and stronger than me. He easily keeps me off the ground, then forces the ball free and runs the other way for a touchdown. It's the first play of the game and I'm crying already.

Before this argument can get far past my initial scream, Dad comes out the front door. Now I'll get my way. "Dad, Scott ripped the ball out of my hands after I caught it. He wouldn't let me go down. That's cheating right?"

"No it's not," Scott defends. "His knee never touched the ground."

"But ..." I am halted by Dad's hand raised at us, saying "Stop!" without a word spoken from him. Walking over to us, he takes the ball from Dallas and looks at me. "You've got to get tougher. Your brothers are tough."

"How? I'm five, the youngest of five and all my brothers have at least eighteen months on me. How do I suddenly get tougher and match them? If you know the way, tell me. I'd love to 'get tougher' and win once in a while. Is that all? Is that the whole message you have for me? There has to be more. I'm waiting," I thought to myself.

Dad flips the ball in his hands a few times, and then clumsily tries to punt it. The ball hits off the side of his foot, heads right and barely makes the gravel about twenty yards away. I've seen him punt the ball three-quarters of the way down the lawn, so I know he can do it. Tonight, he doesn't have the skill for some reason.

Dad doesn't feel like going after the ball. He lets out a long sigh as his eyes seem to wander, trying to find something. He stumbles down to his knees and lies on the grass. "Come here," he states to no one in particular. I've seen this before, so I stay back and let Dallas and Jeff wrestle with him. I'll get the football.

Dad seemed like a massive and powerful man to me as a five-year-old boy. He really only measured about five feet seven inches tall, but weighed in the upper-200's. When he played wrestling with us, he didn't always have the emotional or physical control. Eventually, it seemed Dad would start to get mad about something. The fun turned into a wrestling lesson and when one of us couldn't turn Dad over or put a certain move on him, his voice became stern, his words sharper. At those points, I backed off. I didn't want to play anymore. It was no longer playtime and this was no longer fun.

I caught up to the football as it rested against the tire of Dad's car. I could hear Dad's voice in the background as I began to turn around with the ball. Then I heard a thud as Dad hit the ground, Dallas–his namesake–underneath him. There was another sigh from Dad and faint cries from Dallas.

As always, within a short time, someone was hurt. This time it was Dallas, next time it could be me. I always attributed it to Dad being overweight and not as quick or nimble as he likely once was. His physical conditioning might have contributed, but as I began to recognize the smell of alcohol on his breath, I began to understand there was more behind his lack of body control and his anger.

"Get up!" he shouted to Dallas, then moved his sights onto Jeff. But Jeff was more concerned with Dallas and went to his side to help. Dad, not nimble enough to catch Jeff in a playful attempt to wrestle him, gave up. Exhausted from the few moves he made on the lawn, he rolled onto his side and picked up a can I hadn't noticed before. He took a small drink then heaved it against the front of the house. It made a loud cracking noise as it hit the stone front and sprayed white foam around the small plants Mom had growing there.

"Who wants to get me another beer?" he questioned in a slurred demand.

"I will," I shouted, my legs moving before the words came out. I'll gladly go inside the house even for a few minutes to get away from this all-too-familiar scene.

Dallas wasn't hurt bad, just a bruise this time. It was an accident in all of our eyes, but deep down, it seemed like more. Why couldn't Dad control himself; I thought he was such a good athlete? Why does someone always get hurt?

CHAPTER LESSONS

There's a fine line between play and abuse. For the average person watching a family interact, it can be very hard to detect differences.

Abuse can start slowly, guised in play and build from there. This is the worst kind because the small episodes can become more easily accepted; it becomes normal behavior. It's like the frog put in cool water on a stove. The water heats up slowly so the frog doesn't realize it until it's too late.

The abuse increases in small steps and is excused away by statements like, "He's just had too much to drink," or "He's just not himself today," or "He didn't mean that; Daddy's under a lot of pressure." These are exactly what they seem: excuses.

The blackboards of our lives are being created. If left alone, they will drive us throughout the rest of our lives. Sometimes that's good, but for many, it can be destructive. For many, that which is written on their blackboard needs to be discovered and erased.

ThoughtShredder Moment

In order to become a Bucker, you need to have a process, a method, a way of thinking and acting in order to discover the negative effects created from your blackboard, and then begin erasing them. For some, this comes naturally, but for others it can become a lifetime search—filled with struggle and hardship—not knowing why you keep falling short of what you want and believe you deserve. Your outside mind believes you deserve it, but deep down inside you really don't believe it. The real problem is that you haven't discovered what is blocking that deep down belief from being recognized by you.

You've started with some pre-work of reliving in your mind some of your childhood events. If this has been difficult for you, that's okay. As you follow through with the full ThoughtShredder process, it will become easier and easier to uncover some of those deep memories.

Awareness of the chaos is the first step in ThoughtShredder. Buckers first have to recognize events, circumstances or statements that created chaos or limiting beliefs within them. By doing your pre-work, you will begin to remember these events.

The easiest way to recognize a chaos event or a limiting belief is to check your stomach. When you relive the event, are you overwhelmed with a sense of comfort and love? If so, this is not chaos. When you relive the event, do you begin to feel an uneasy feeling in your stomach? Do you start to feel a tightening in your body and do you have a desire to move on to the next memory?

At this moment, many of you will put this book down. You'll tell yourself that this isn't what you really need. You'll come up with an abundance of excuses to forget all about this. First, that's okay. You're not ready yet. When you're ready, you'll come back to this.

Keep in mind that the things we run from control us. Once we face them and stand up to them, we can be free from their control.

For many of you, that is exactly where I want you to be. You've done it. You've hit on a memory that is affecting you in ways you don't realize, but the effect is not good. Deep down you know it and your heart is telling you that the belief created by this memory is not right. You're better than that. You deserve more, and you do. It's time to recognize these events and write them down.

ACTION PLAN

Buy yourself a new tablet or a journal; create a special folder in your computer for documenting, or use the back of each chapter in this book to document your journey. Continue your memory exercises and document your childhood memories that affected you most. Do these in a quiet place where you are not distracted. Get deeper and deeper with your memories. Each time you feel that uneasy feeling, write it down in that new journal or document it in that special folder in your computer. Write down the event that you are remembering. Under that, write down the emotions you are feeling. You may be feeling sad or lonely or scared. Write that down. If you can't tell exactly what you are feeling, write down what is happening in your body. Are you feeling tightness anywhere? Do you feel like running away? Are there tears in your eyes? Whatever it is, write it down.

If you make it through this step in the ThoughtShredder process, you are well on your way.

MY JOURNEY

3

DISCIPLINE

The kids are all in bed as the morning sun begins to peek over the thin clouds that mask the horizon. I take a few moments to look out the twins' bedroom window in awe of the morning scene that appears painted on the window. I savor this moment, sipping my coffee, taking in the peaceful silence. I know that too soon it will be broken by the sounds of kids hustling to get breakfast eaten, clothes picked out, hair and teeth brushed and backpacks loaded up as they prepare for another day of school.

Through the windows I can see the emerging sky just over the rooftops of the neighborhood houses. I screen my view to imagine the scene without the rooftops. This is what it looked like when I was a child waking up on school day mornings. No other buildings in view, just wide open fields with patches of trees sprinkled in. The sky seemed to stretch forever.

Back then, it was customary for me to hear Mom's wake-up call, rustle in bed for a few minutes, and then head downstairs for breakfast. On my way down the steps, I would grab a blanket to wrap around me. On winter mornings the blanket wasn't enough. I'd sit down in front of the furnace vent waiting for the next blast of warm air to smother me. The sky would be black until I started my walk down the long driveway to the school bus. That's when that incredible sky would hit me.

A light chuckle escapes me now as I think about my responsibility to wake my children up this morning. They too will grab blankets and wrap themselves up in them as they sit at the kitchen table waiting for their breakfast. Today it's waffles *fresh* from the toaster.

Before I can take my eyes off the window scene, I feel a gentle hug on my leg. It's Carson. He woke up early and is standing at my side, burying his face into my thigh likely wishing it was his pillow. I reach down and firmly press him harder to me. That unbreakable bond is reinforced.

Carson is in kindergarten and growing closer and closer to me each day. He loves to wrestle with me at night, jump on the trampoline with me during the day and can't wait to help Dad fix anything around the house. He'll be disappointed in that later as he realizes Dad's limitations on fixing most things.

"Will I still be this close to Owen when he's five?" I ask myself silently. Owen is the fifth child in our family and the youngest. The same spot I hold among my brothers and sister. Will I love him the same, spoil him because he's the youngest, or like my dad, feel overwhelmed and burdened by him? Will Owen feel the same as I did when I was five? That familiar scene in the laundry room of our old house comes back to me …

"Misty!" I shout as I run my five-year-old body through the front door leading me out of our kitchen and into the laundry room. The cold of the cement floor in the laundry room seeps through my socks to my feet. The chill runs through my entire body. But Misty is there to warm me.

Misty is our German shepherd dog. She's very young, but looks full grown to me. I throw my arms around her black and white neck to give her a big hug, savoring the warmth. Excited to have a companion, Misty licks my face and rubs her head on me almost knocking me over. It must be a game to her, so I play along and wrestle with her.

Playtime is quickly interrupted as Dad walks in holding his hunting gun. He's wiping the gun with a rag creating a dark black shine on it. The smell of the liquid he's using penetrates my nose, almost stinging it. I'm intrigued enough to stop playing with Misty for a moment and stand by Dad's side watching. Misty, still excited about playing continues to push me until I bump up against Dad.

I looked down at Misty to try to stop her, but was stopped in my tracks by a stunning sensation. It was one of those moments where all your senses are shocked and seem to scatter away from you. A moment of hesitation goes by as you try to corral all of them back in their places. In the next split second as your senses come back, pain is the first one to return.

I felt the sting across my face and put my hand over my mouth to feel a trickle of warm fluid. I looked at my hand to see a mixture of blood and tears. The blood was coming from my nose and the tears were rolling down my cheeks. I didn't have time to create these, they just happened in an instant.

That is the first memory I have of physically feeling his anger. I don't remember anything about that incident after that, but likely Dad made some comment about how I should stop crying or he'd give me something to cry about. I was five and Dad had come close to crossing the line, or had he crossed it already?

It didn't take long for me to feel further effects of Dad's methods. Whether it was because of the drinking or just his temper, we all learned his short fuse. The problem I had was in not understanding what triggered it. What did I do or say this time that got him so mad?

Having Misty next to me at the time now seems a bit ironic to me. She was our family dog, but was also used to breed other German shepherds. Dad would raise and train the dogs to a certain level, then sell them to the Army. I loved having all the dogs around. The puppies were so cuddly and they licked our faces and hands. They jumped all over us whenever we came home from school or stepped outside at first light of morning. They seemed so excited to see us. This was possibly my first experience with unconditional love—outside my mother.

Dad had a knack for raising them. He knew how to manage them with a stern voice and swift slap. He knew their trigger points and they responded quickly. At one point, a man brought over an albino German shepherd that he could not control. The dog was known to be friendly at some points, but could quickly turn mean and attack without provocation. Dad's reputation for controlling dogs got back to this man and he asked Dad for help. Hearing that story gave me a sense of pride; my dad was better than anyone else this man knew at controlling dogs. The problem was that Dad also had to raise children.

Raising children is so much different than raising dogs. A stern voice is certainly acceptable, but a hand, a fist and a strap: these tools are not acceptable. I wonder if Dad knew there was a difference? It seemed he did, but he thought the temperament required to raise children took too much effort. Instead of putting in the effort, the same method was used to suit both. That method created some respect. I respected Dad. The problem was that I feared him more. Fear used in raising a child is like pounding a nail with a wrench. The tool is ill suited for the job. It will work in a pinch, but is not sustainable. Dad's method worked well on dogs, but not on children.

That day in the laundry room opened my eyes. I was to see a whole new world from that point on. I'm not sure if the world was already there and I was just too young and naïve to see it before, or if events were about to suddenly grow out of control. Was Dad always like this and that slap brought it to my consciousness, or did something change in him? Did one slap make all the others that much easier for him?

Some part of me was searching to understand why he would do that. Mom never did that. Why would he? For many of those early years I was longing for the same type of love and affection that Mom gave. Dad was proving he didn't have it; yet at times he could be so gentle with those dogs. Did he have love, but not know how to show it? Or did he not have love?

CHAPTER LESSONS

Abuse starts with the first act and becomes easier each time. Recognize it with the first act and stop it.

Discipline is not abuse. The root of discipline is disciple—to teach or train. Abuse means to deceive or mislead. One has a purpose to teach while the other wants to control and harm.

If there is no explanation of what was wrong and what should be done in the future, there can be no discipline. As a parent, we owe being a disciple to our children to teach them the proper behavior.

Children are unique, precious human beings. They are not animals to be trained, nor are they miniature adults. Each needs to be taught cause and effect. When a mistake is made, discipline the child with intent and show the right way.

ThoughtShredder Moment

An abuser doesn't jump into abuse; he slowly develops it through small actions that begin to build onto each other until he doesn't even recognize the difference between the abuse and the discipline.

You might jump into the ThoughtShredder process, but the journey to becoming a Bucker is not a quick-fix. It starts with simple steps that build on each other, identifying and erasing the events that make up your blackboard. You will feel guilty at times. You will feel lost at times. You will feel like giving up. This is the time to push through even harder.

I will never forget my high school chemistry class. The teacher asked the class a question about chemistry and several hands went up. Seeing that my friend Mark was not paying attention, the teacher called his name and said, "What is your answer, Mark?"

Mark immediately threw out his answer, "Because steam has six times the energy of boiling water."

"That is correct," the teacher responded, "but that's not the question I asked."

The class burst into laughter at Mark's expense and a memory was burned to my blackboard.

What I learned is that it is pretty easy to get water to boil, but it is still water. Sure it's hotter and it's jumping around a lot in the pot, but it is still water. To make it change into steam, you have to be willing to put in a lot more energy. Starting the process of ThoughtShredder is pretty easy. Making lasting change in your life takes a lot more energy. The rewards of the change carry a lot more energy also.

As you continue recognizing events that shaped your life, keep pushing to dig deeper and deeper to uncover more memories. The effort you put in will pay off big.

Keep in mind that you will have great memories also. These are important to keep and to relive at times. They still create joy in your life. As you remember these times, write them down in your journal and write down the great emotions you feel as you remember them.

ACTION PLAN

Keep pushing through the tough times. Go back and re-read some of your initial memories and see if new ones emerge from them. As new ones come, write them down. Also write down the good memories and the wonderful emotions you associate with them. This will become a journal of your childhood that will allow you to separate the negative events from the positive events. This will be important as we move through the process.

Think about the steam you are generating for your change.

My Journey

_____

_____

_____

_____

_____

_____

_____

_____

_____

_____

_____

_____

_____

_____

_____

_____

_____

_____

_____

_____

_____

4

TRUE EMOTIONS

With my wife Tracy home and watching the twins, I can take a quick trip to the store to pick up some ingredients for cookies. The kids love to make cut-out cookies with me.

Together we will make the dough and then roll it out on the kitchen island. Each child will get to cut out any shape they want from the dough. The cookies take twelve minutes to bake and twenty-five more to cool off. While they cool, we make the frosting and let the kids each pick out their favorite coloring to add. Individual bowls of frosting are made and colored for each. At that point, it's almost time to have a frosting party.

The kids will pick out their cookie from the cooling rack and set up their spot at the table. The set-up will include their bowl of frosting, a spreading utensil—generally a butter knife—plate and plenty of napkins. On special occasions, we add sprinkles to the mix and get the vacuum cleaner ready.

Today, it's just colored frosting we're going to use, but we need vanilla and sour cream to make the cookie dough.

"Does anyone want to go to the store with me?" I shout.

Megan jumps at the chance. "I'll go. Can we get a treat?"

"Not this time," is my disappointing response. "We're making cookies. That's a treat right there."

She seems satisfied and hops into the back of the truck. She loves to be unique. It's her favorite characteristic. She frequently says, "I love to be unique and make people smile."

We back out of the driveway and I ask Megan my typical question, "What's great about today?"

She begins her response with her typical, "Well ..."

But she is cut off by me swerving the Envoy to the left side of the road and back again. Both hands grip the steering wheel tight as I gain control again. The phone that was in my lap is now somewhere on the floor of the passenger side of the truck. As I look through the rear view mirror, I see the black dog sprinting across the neighbor's driveway. I'm not sure whose dog it is, but it just missed my front right tire. My heart is pounding out of control, but at least I am back in control of the truck.

"Where did that come from?" Megan asks not really looking for answer. Then she continues on with her response to my original question. "Anyway ..."

She talks on, but my focus moves internally. It's been awhile since I've felt that jarring motion of a vehicle swerving from one side of the road to another. The first time was when I was six ...

Dad was sick that morning with the "flu", Mom had told us, so he was sleeping in. He seemed to have the "flu" on most weekends. It took a long time for me to figure out that these sleep-in times for Dad weren't always the flu.

I was still angered by the scene from the night before; Dad was driving us home from our cousins' house late in the night. He was drunk and tickling Mom while he drove. The car swerved to the opposite lane each time he reached over and playfully tried to tickle her. It started out as fun to him, I guess this was his way of saying he was in the mood. But eventually, Mom would get concerned, scared about getting into an accident. Don't tell my dad that. He was in control.

I was in the backseat and watching the car move from roadside to roadside with lights coming from the other direction at us in the dead of night. "Please just get us home. I want to be out of this car," I prayed to myself.

When Mom asked him to stop because he was scaring the kids, Dad took it as rejection. Mom's resistance had worn on Dad and his playfulness turned to anger: the first and seemingly favorite of his emotions. Soon the bad words came out. At least he had two hands on the wheel and we were only a mile or so from home. I could see our yard light over the field. We'd be home and safe, safe from the car swerving anyway, not safe from Dad.

Of course, Mom bringing up the kids to support her request for him to stop meant it was our fault. "Get up and get to bed," he hollered at us with a quick hand to ensure we heard it. I did hear it, and rubbing my cheek, went up the stairs to my bed. I was more concerned about Mom than myself and made sure to walk slowly up the stairs as if that would diminish his anger. What was he going to do to her? I went upstairs to bed, but couldn't sleep listening to the raised voices below, sometimes muffled, other times graphically clear.

She'd try to calm him with, "You're going to wake up the kids." But that was pointless.

"Fine, I don't care, I'll get everyone of them up right now," was his response.

I'm not sure what that was supposed to accomplish other than to display the power and control he thought he had. Finally, doors slammed and the words became muffled as I fell asleep. No apparent damage this time, but I still felt uneasy in the morning.

When Mom woke up, a light bruise appeared on her cheek. I noticed a hole in the wall outside Mom and Dad's bedroom. "What's that," I asked? A slight pause by Mom was followed by a made up answer to cover up the fact that Dad punched a hole in the wall in his rage from last night. Lucky for him, he didn't hit a stud and break his hand. Lucky for us it was just the wall.

CHAPTER LESSONS

Control seems to be the first need of the abuser; he or she must have power rather than influence. Without power they feel no control; they feel vulnerable. Vulnerability seems to be the enemy of the abuser; he or she never wants you to see the real person.

Anger is the first emotion he or she displays; even if the real emotion is a feeling of rejection, frustration, loneliness or hurt, it is displayed as anger.

Alcohol is not the initiator of abuse, nor can it be used as an excuse. It might be tied to it, but there is a deeper problem. To me, alcohol becomes the pacifier; it allows the abuser to forget the current moment by numbing it away.

ThoughtShredder Moment

PHASE ONE:
THE RECOGNITION PHASE

Part of The Recognition Phase of ThoughtShredder is recognizing why the other person acted the way he or she did, or why they continue to act that way. There may be people in your life who are inflicting abuse or people who are supplying you with limited beliefs through their comments. Recognize who these people are; identify them by name. Once you know who they are, understand why they act the way they do.

With family members, I suggest getting into some of the details and really understanding them. Sit down with them and have a private conversation about their life. Ask them about how they grew up. What was it like as a child? You'll be surprised at how many people enjoy talking about themselves and reminiscing about the past. As it was for you, there will be moments of uneasiness, moments when he or she becomes uncomfortable with parts of the story. Keep listening and let them share everything they want to share. If that person is no longer with you, talk to close family members and really try to understand how they grew up. You'll be surprised at what you learn.

If you are dealing with people outside your immediate family who have had negative effects on you, tread lightly. Their willingness to share and their sense of obligation to you might be very different than that of a family member.

This part of The Recognition Phase includes understanding that everyone has a blackboard that created who they are. Recognize that their childhood likely wasn't perfect and it wasn't their fault. You might discover specific details that allow you to really empathize with this person or you might only get vague references to their childhood. The most important part for you is to recognize that their blackboard exists just as yours does. The unfortunate thing for them is they likely haven't found a process to become a Bucker like you have.

ACTION PLAN

As you remember your childhood events, identify those in your life—then and now—who have had a negative impact on you. Write the names of these individuals in your journal next to the memories and the feelings you get from those memories. Sit down with them or their family members and listen to their stories. Build an understanding within you.

Keep recognizing and being aware of your blackboard.

My Journey

5

SEEMINGLY
INSIGNIFICANT MOMENTS

It's a new morning and the steady trickle of rain on the roof and windows creates a calming rhythm that puts the twins to sleep for me. It looks like it will be a long nap for the twins. I carry each boy upstairs to his room, kiss him on his cheek and wrap him in the warm blankets of his crib. Their closed eyes and gentle breathing remind me of the peace in my world today. I wonder if there is any feeling as great as this. As I walk out of their bedroom, quietly closing the door, I peer down the hallway hearing the giggles of my girls. They are both in their room playing dress-up.

Megan skips down the hallway past me and heads down the steps. "Where are you going?" I ask.

My question stops her in her tracks and she stands on the small platform on our steps. The staircase goes straight up from the front door for nine steps then turns ninety degrees before adding four more steps to the second floor. At the turn is a square platform about three feet by three feet. The kids like to use it as a landing point for their jumps from the top step.

"I'm going downstairs to get some make-up. We're going to play dress-up with make-up," she states very matter-of-factly. I'm not sure her mother would approve of that, but my attention is diverted from her statement and she continues down the steps.

I turn to go down the steps also, but I am momentarily halted. I put my hand on the railing and trace the steps with my eyes from the top, past the turn at step four and all the way down to bottom.

The small platform after step four reminds me of the platform at the top of our steps at my childhood home. The house I grew up in is so much different than the house I live in now. Yet simple things like the steps, crayon colored walls and that platform remind me so much of the old house. My response to Megan will have to wait as I think back on that old house …

Mom was stressed, as most parents would be who delivered five children within a seven-year span. She was the primary caregiver as was customary during that time. Dad was supposed to be the breadwinner and Mom the housewife, but it didn't turn out quite that simple. Mom took care of us, the house cleaning and the cooking, but she also worked a full-time job for as long as I can remember. She worked in a factory during the day and Dad worked night shift in the computer room of a different manufacturing plant.

I remember Dad taking us to his work one night. That was so fun. We rode an elevator for the first time and saw these really neat machines that held candy in them. All you had to do was put a coin in the slot and candy fell out—my first vending machine. Dad had the coolest job in the world.

For some reason, with both of them working, they still complained about not having any money. I'm not sure where it all went, but I remember Dad taking another job on weekends tending bar. I'm not sure if he needed to take the job or if he just enjoyed being in bars. Either way, that job ended up costing more than it paid. On one night, it cost him his family.

The house we lived in wasn't very big when I compared it with some of my friends' houses, especially those who lived on a farm. Our house seemed big enough for me as a child. I have no idea of the square footage. It had three bedrooms and one bathroom. Two of the bedrooms were upstairs and one bedroom downstairs. The stairs were thirteen carpeted steps straight up, with silvery metal edges that seemed to be there to hold the carpet in place. Once you got to the top of the stairs, you either turned left into the boys' room, where I slept on the top bunk, or you turned right into my parents' room. There were no hallways upstairs, just a platform at the top of the steps that separated the two bedrooms. That platform served as stage for one of the most dramatic events of my childhood.

The best part of sleeping upstairs was when Mom would vacuum while we were in bed. That low humming sound was the perfect melody to put me to sleep. The sound calmed me for some reason. It seemed a combination of the steady hum and the knowing that Mom was just downstairs. I was safe and warm in my bed. That would not last.

"Dr. J dribbles right, spins past the defender, now switches hands. He fakes left, drives right, pumps once and slams the ball. What an unbelievable play by Dr. J!" That's my commentary on my own move as I pretend to be Dr. J, Julius Irving.

I'm not Dr. J, I'm only seven and I'm not on a real basketball court or even using a real basketball. I'm in the dining room holding onto a roll of wrapped up masking tape I formed into a ball. This is one of the great games we play when Mom and Dad are out. Oatmeal containers get cut in half and become makeshift basketball hoops. We tape them to the archways leading to the living room on one side and the kitchen on the other side. We slide the table over a bit and the dining room becomes the basketball court. Even though it's not really ten feet high, I still can't really dunk a ball into the oatmeal containers, but a child's imagination can do anything.

Scott sees the "court" and wants to play now too. We spend an hour or so playing a few games. Arguments ensue and we quit for awhile, but they are quickly forgotten or overshadowed by the fun of playing basketball and we pick it back up again.

Dallas and Jeff are in the living room playing music loudly. Jeff sits on the couch and rocks to the music. He's like the rest of us; he just feels a need to move when he hears music. His movement is to rock while Dallas and I like to dance. That's what Dallas is doing now, dancing. He stands in the middle of the living room facing the large wall mirror and dances to whatever song is on. Most times he holds a pretend microphone and sings along.

The house is filled with chaos and the music blares, Dallas dances around, Jeff rocks, Scott and I jump around the dining room playing basketball and wrestling for a runaway ball of tape. With all of this fun, the night will fly by; and it does.

"It's time to go to bed guys," Dallas states, breaking up the fun.

"But it's Friday and Mom's not home yet," I plead.

"Mom's meeting Dad out tonight, so they won't be home for awhile. It's time for bed."

Dad was working his typical second shift and was then heading to his part-time job tending bar. Mom and my sister Julie, the oldest of us kids, went out to meet him. With Mom out for the night, no vacuum cleaning put me to sleep. Even without that, by 3:00 a.m., I was plenty deep in sleep.

I imagine that I heard Mom and Dad come home, but like any other night that they went out, I likely heard the door open and close, then just rolled over again and fell back to sleep. By about 3:00 this night, the noises became way too loud for me to just roll over.

I woke in the top bunk to what sounded like my Mom's voice, but not the same type of voice I had been accustomed to. This voice was scared, hurt and fighting back tears. I perked up in my bunk and looked over my brother to see what was happening. Through the open bedroom door, I could see that platform at the top of the steps. The hallway light became a spotlight for the whole scene.

Dad had Mom by the back of neck with one hand and held her elbow in his other hand. He was forcing her from their bedroom to that small platform. Mom had tears coming down her face, rolling off cheeks that seemed too red for just tears.

"That son of a bitch hit her again," I thought in a brief moment of anger. But anger only lasted a second as fear quickly took over. The fear I could see in my Mom's face penetrated me to places in my body I didn't know existed. I never felt fear in my fingertips before, but that's how deeply penetrating that initial scene was.

Dad moved her body with little effort. He had total control. She was facing us with her side toward the steps. I saw Mom's eyes glance to the side and down the steps. That made it even more real for me. She was looking down at her likely destination, wondering how it would feel; how would she protect herself as she went down; how many bones would be broken; would she survive; and who would take care of her kids if she didn't? In that moment, I was wondering the same.

I wanted to storm off that bunk and tackle him, then pick him back up, spin him around and send him down those steps. As he lay at the bottom, I would stand over him and ask and him how that felt. At seven years old, that too was just fantasy like playing Julius Irving.

Dad was making some angry comments to her, threatening her in some way that I couldn't quite make out. Then Mom's voice came out as clear to my ears today as it was back then.

"Dallas, help your mother," she begged to her now thirteen-year-old son. She had to call on a boy who weighed all of about 100 pounds to help her from a man who weighed well over 200. "Dallas, help your mother." Four simple words that could be spoken at any time to request help with the garden, the dishes, shoveling snow from the sidewalk or carrying groceries from the car. Those are things a thirteen-year-old should be helping his mother with. He shouldn't be helping to save his mother's life from a mad man who's had too much to drink and can't control his jealousy.

Dallas jumped from his lower bunk and was at her side with two steps. Hope came to me in an instant and was dashed in the next. As quickly as Dallas got to her side, a hard backhand from Dad sent him right back into his bunk. I gave up. Dallas is the oldest and strongest boy in the family. If he can't help her, none of us can.

I laid back down, held my hands over my ears, then kicked and whined like a child throwing a tantrum for not getting a piece of candy. The kicking was out of frustration. The whining was to ensure I didn't hear any more. "Just tell me when it's all over," I thought.

Scott shook me, and then in an innocent and likely caring way, asked me what was wrong. When a child throws a tantrum, it's understandable to wonder why. It worked to stop me, but only long enough for me to wonder what scene he was watching. In my mind, I asked, "Do you understand that our father is about to throw our mother down the steps? Do you hear her pleas for help? Are you in the same world I am in?" I'm sure he was in my world, but like me, didn't know how to react.

I looked back at Mom, still being controlled like a rag doll by my dad and saw for a brief moment the hope leave her face also. She was giving up, resigning to the fact that she would somehow end up in a ball at the bottom of the steps.

Through the chaos, the screams, the crying children and the threats by my dad, came the simplest of sounds, the same sound that started this night for me. It wasn't another loud voice taking control, it wasn't the sound of two bodies struggling to set someone free, nor the crashing sound of someone falling. It was the sound of a door slamming.

It was the front door and Julie had slammed it. Julie was Dad's soft spot and even in his state of rage and drunkenness, somehow he understood what that sound meant. Julie had run away. Tired of this scene, fed up with all the anger and all the pain, she left. She slammed the front door and ran as fast and as far as she could.

That sound saved a lot that night. What was saved, we'll never know for sure, but I'm confident the scene was only going to get worse if something didn't happen to stop it. It was clear that the efforts of four young boys weren't going to impact it. That seemingly insignificant moment of slamming a door became an incredibly significant moment in all of our lives.

As that sound penetrated all of us, it quickly turned the house to silence. Dad let go of Mom and allowed her to walk herself down the stairs. We all followed behind her down the stairs and out the front door into the black night. We called for Julie, but got no answer. All we could see were the faint lights from the neighbor's yard a half-mile away. All we could hear was the wind blowing through the trees and the dog whimpering for attention.

I remember it being a black night with few stars. I noticed no temperature as I walked around the outside of the house wearing nothing but a t-shirt and underwear. I had no sense of whether we would find Julie that night or not. I'm not sure I really cared. I knew that Mom was safe. She was scared, worried, trying to appear strong to us, but she was safe for now. That was all I really cared about. I thought to myself, "Let's just keep walking around this house; let's not find Julie. If we keep looking, we won't have to go back inside. If we look all night, we won't have to go back inside until the sun comes up. Things always look different when the sun's up." That's what I wanted, but I knew we'd have to go back in eventually.

Mom called us all in and told us to go back to bed. I walked in tired and scared, but relieved that the earlier scene was over. As I entered the kitchen, my eyes would see a sight that further displayed the unbelievable gall of my father. There was Dad in a t-shirt sitting at the table having heated up a leftover steak and some cottage fries. He was eating.

I remember wondering what kind of monster can even think of eating at this time. Then as I walked past him, he told me to get him a towel. "Get your own damn towel," is what I was thinking. "Here, how about a knife to your heart?" is what I wanted to do. Instead, I walked to the towel drawer, pulled one out and set it on the table. I walked past him again to go upstairs and he said no thank you nor intimated an apology. He simply said, "Julie will be okay."

"I don't care about Julie right now. I care about Mom. I wonder what's going to happen next time? I wonder if I go to bed will she be here in the morning and if she is, will she be alive? I want to sleep in the living room with her and know that she's here. I want you to get the hell out of here and never come back. Better yet, I'd like to beat the hell out of you right now so you know what it feels like. And I wonder why God allows someone like you to be here." That is what I said to myself. To him, I said nothing. I just walked away, up the stairs again to go to bed, wondering when I would have to live this all over again. When would he lose control again?

It turned out that Julie ran to a friend's house some three or four miles away. She ran in the dead of night, crossing a main highway and fields, escaping the annoyance of the country dogs, rustling the neighbors' horses at one point and stopping by their pool for a drink.

I don't know her intent that night or if she realized with that desperate act that she had stopped the madness for a moment. I wonder if she slept at all that night or if she sat up waiting for the knock on the door from Mom or Dad searching for her. Or would that knock be from the police giving her the bad news? I wonder if she sat up thinking about the events and wondering if Mom was still alive or if he followed through this time. I wonder now if she even realizes that seemingly insignificant moment wasn't so insignificant.

I didn't get hurt this time and yet that night had a greater impact on me than any belt, hand or fist could have. That night created more mental and emotional scars than his hand could have. That night Dad didn't just cross the line; he leaped the fence. He went so far past the point that any child could forget or forgive. And I went to a place where I thought I would never return from either. That place was where I no longer considered him my father. He could leave now, never return and I'd be happy; I'd encourage it. I'd even help him pack is bags. I didn't realize how close my wish would come to being true.

I don't know how many times the pictures from that scene have played out in my head. I don't know how many times since that I wondered if Mom would survive the night. I don't know how many times I wondered what other fathers were like. And I might never know how significant the effects of that event have played a role in my growth or delay in growth. What I do know is that tears fill my eyes with each memory. And with each picture I wonder what makes a man become a monster.

You might think that this was the worst event of my life, but it wasn't. I remember the details fairly vividly of this event, mostly because of the possible consequences. I was within a few moments of potentially losing my mother … at the hands of my father. But it wasn't the worst memory I have. Another event sticks in my mind even more vividly and stings my senses with even greater sensation, not because of the images this time, but because of the sounds that I heard.

CHAPTER LESSONS

Don't give up; don't quit. I was ready to give up until that front door slammed shut. Do whatever is in your power to stop the madness, even if that means running away to get help.

Just because you cannot be part of the solution does not make you part of the problem. I often blamed myself for not stopping that scene—for being too small and too weak to help.

Seemingly insignificant moments (SIMS) can create the solution. You never know when a simple act can have an incredible influence on the outcome or where that solution will exist. Slamming that door suddenly became the solution.

No one knows exactly when and where the blackboard starts; however, it is evident that many events reinforce the writings on the board. As abuse continues, the writings go deeper and deeper having more and more affect on us.

Take every incident in your life as an opportunity to learn and overcome. Don't blame yourself; don't feel guilty. Ask yourself, "What can I learn? What is God trying to teach me here?" Then wait for the answer.

ThoughtShredder Moment

Phase Two:
The Rid Phase

You have been going through The Recognition Phase of ThoughtShredder and are likely uncovering events from your past that you had hoped to keep buried. You are also discovering that the people who hurt you most were likely hurt by others as they grew up. You might be wondering why I am asking you to go through the pain of remembering. The answer is in Phase Two of ThoughtShredder: ridding yourself of these events.

As we discussed, the blackboard of our lives appears set. Events and beliefs based on them appear to be etched and permanent, but that is not true. It is true that we cannot go back and "unlive" the events. However, we can go back and remove the beliefs we have associated with the events. To do this we rid ourselves of those beliefs.

The importance of The Rid Phase cannot be overstated. You have likely heard many people mention positive self-talk, affirmations, intentions, etc. all of which refer to building a belief in yourself by repeatedly telling yourself how good you are. For instance, if you want to be more confident, you will follow the affirmation process by stating multiple times a day that you are a very confident person. The intent is to build a new belief within you.

I love this process as part of a total program. My problem with it alone is that the new belief is being built on top of old beliefs. As you know, a new house built on an old and worn out foundation will still crumble. Your old beliefs are the old foundation and building new beliefs on top of them will cause the new beliefs to eventually crumble. The Rid Phase first removes the old foundation allowing you to more effectively build a new foundation on new beliefs that do not restrict you.

For me, the stairs incident between my mother and father created a belief in me that when times get tough, quit. I learned to hide during crucial times. If victory didn't seem in sight, quit. That doesn't work in life; life hands you too many moments of resistance. To overcome this, I had to rid myself of that belief so I could effectively act differently in tough times.

ACTION PLAN

Go back to your journal and pick out three events that you want to get rid of from a belief side: three events that created beliefs you no longer want to serve you. Go to a new page in your journal and write down that first event along with the belief you associate with it. Stare at that belief; let it sink into you; feel the uneasiness of it. Feel it intently. Now rip that page out of your journal and tear it into shreds. Don't just crumble it up, rip it up. Feel the passion, anger and excitement of tearing that belief up. Go to the next event you chose and do the same action. Complete this for all three. Tomorrow, do the same thing until that feeling of uneasiness you get when reading it diminishes. Then you know you're ready for Phase Three.

Enjoy this activity. The more fun and passion you put into this phase, the more effective you will be as a Bucker.

6

BLAMING YOURSELF

Carson and I walk down the stairs of our new house and into the kitchen to get him some apple juice. Carson loves apple juice. My two older daughters loved grape juice at his age, but he's been a fan of apple juice since he was a toddler. We are a frugal family so we buy juice in the frozen concentrate containers and make it ourselves in this really cool pitcher. The pitcher has a handle on the top of the cover that can be pulled up and pushed down in a plunger motion. The insert attached moves up and down inside the juice container creating a swirling affect and mixing the juice. It's one of those simple, yet great creations I wish I had invented.

Carson pulls his stool up to the freezer door, pulls down a frozen juice container and sets it on the kitchen island to thaw. For the next 30 minutes he asks, "Is it ready yet, Dad? Is it ready yet? Is it ready yet? How about now? Is it ready now?" He's learning patience.

Once it's ready, Carson puts the pitcher on the table and opens up the juice container. He pours the concentrate into the pitcher, and then fills the now-empty juice container with water from the faucet. He dumps the water into the pitcher with the concentrate and repeats this until the pitcher is full.

"It's done, Dad; oh wait. It needs just a little more," he states with excitement, his little eyes wide open and focused on the next bit of water, trying to ensure he doesn't spill any.

When the container is finally filled to his satisfaction, I put the top on that has the little plunger part. "Can I do it, Dad?" Carson begs.

"You bet." He pulls the plunger up and down watching the water and juice mix together with bubbles and splashes of golden light mixing as well.

I think the enjoyment of making the juice is more satisfying to him than actually drinking it. I enjoy the process and the time with him.

Before he's completely finished with his juice, Carson hears his sisters calling for him and he runs through the living room trying to get back to the stairs. In his excitement, he trips, falls to the floor and spills his new juice on the living room carpet. A burst of anger grips me immediately and dissipates just as quickly as I watch Carson's reaction.

He grabs his leg in pain and shows a slight grimace on his face. Then he looks at the growing wet spot on the carpet and realizes his mistake. He turns to me, ignoring any physical pain, and says, "Sorry, Daddy."

He's a tough kid who rarely cries—a quality he gets from his Uncle Dallas who I rarely saw cry while we were kids. Carson's earnest apology and recognition of his mistake appease me. Instead of cleaning the mess, I fall on the floor next to him and begin to tickle him. He laughs loudly and wiggles his body around completely forgetting his pain. I lose sense of the power I have and forget that he's just a little boy. Even laughing too long hurts him. Suddenly his laughter turns to pleas to me. He manages to get out two words, "No, Daddy!"

The words strike my heart deeply and instantly. I am compelled by some other force to stop and hug him immediately. "No, Daddy! No, Daddy!" The words ring in my ears. I shake my head trying to rid myself of them, but I can't. Carson's words remind me of the same two simple words from Dallas' mouth that I cannot shake, nor can I escape the memory they bring …

The stairs incident was quickly dismissed in our family, never to be talked about again. Julie came back home, Mom and Dad went back to work and the rest of us kids continued with chores for the summer. Dallas and Jeff helped my uncle bale hay, while Scott tagged along and learned the trade. I was at home learning to clean and take care of laundry. I would be out in fields soon. Everything went along throughout the rest of that summer as though this incident never happened. It was an unwritten rule that we just bury that memory and move on. And we did, but nothing seemed to feel right anymore.

As fall approached, cool temperatures began creeping in and the sky darkened much earlier. Outside play ended earlier than we liked, supper seemed later, and bedtime as always, came way too soon. It was on one of these cool nights when the sky was already black, but I was wide awake, that I heard the two words that bring tears to my eyes today.

"Time to come in!" came the call. It was Mom yelling out the front door into the early evening darkness. She couldn't see us playing catch with the ball and we could hardly see her either. She knew we were there and that we would quickly come in. But I wasn't ready to be done playing.

"Go get it!" I yelled as I threw the ball over Scott's head to the end of the lawn. We both ran to get it, but I had a head start and beat him to it. I jumped on the ball and we both rolled around on the lawn for a few minutes more.

"Kids, get in here!" was now the shout from a much louder voice. It was Dad this time. We didn't come in from the first call and now he meant business.

"Stay clear of Dad tonight," I thought as I came in the house and took off my sweatshirt. I was careful taking it off ensuring I didn't drop the ball I brought in with me. I threw the sweatshirt onto the steps and ran to the living room to continue playing.

"Supper's ready," Mom declared, while chairs began to fill up.

Still busy playing with the football, throwing it in the air, and catching it, I see Dallas still in the living room and figure I can play a little longer. He is listening to the record player: one of his favorite activities.

"Turn off the record and get in here," I hear from my dad.

Dallas quickly moves to the record player to turn it off. This is my chance. I can play little brother and annoy my big brother a bit. That's what I do best and it's fun for me.

I yell to Dallas, "Catch!" and throw the ball too early and too high for him to reasonably catch. Then I run quickly out of the room.

Dallas missed the ball and it landed on the record player. The handle of the record player moved across the record and made a brief, but irritating sound. Dallas scrambled to get the ball while simultaneously picking up the arm of the player. He moved quickly and nervously to set the handle back in its off position and shut the player off. But there was no way to be quick enough.

Dad heard the sound from the kitchen and saw Dallas by the record player. Dad was off his chair before Dallas could move. Dallas quickly turned toward our approaching father and began defending himself about the ball. What Dad saw was Dallas by the record player and a ball in his hand. No more evidence was needed. Dallas was guilty and deserving of punishment.

It was one of his quick reactions that seemingly made no sense to us. There was no explanation of what we did wrong, and no teaching of the correct actions. There was only swift, angry retribution.

Dallas was grabbed by the arm and taken to the couch. Dad had him pull his pants down while Dad took off his belt. At that moment, I hid in the kitchen. I didn't hide from the possibility of being spanked myself. I hid from the event, trying to escape the sounds, but to no avail. The sounds came through.

I could hear the belt hit and Dallas crying. Those were sounds I had heard many times, too many, and I was growing used to them. The words that Dallas cried while being spanked were the sounds that pierced my eardrums like a needle and burned my heart like an iron. The words that Dallas uttered in desperation were just two—"No, Daddy."

He was not crying these words out of just pain and frustration; this was pleading. This was a boy trapped without hope, helpless against the brutality. He was not being spanked; he was being tortured. This was not a lesson being taught, but the rage of a grown man being let out on an innocent and naïve boy.

"No, Daddy! No, Daddy!" he kept pleading with each slap of the belt. And with each utterance I could feel the sting of the belt myself. I was witness to the sounds while my closed eyes could not stop the images from playing in my mind. I pictured the cruelty happening and Dallas squirming to get away without any chance for escape. Dad was too powerful.

When it all ended, Dallas walked past me, up the stairs, and lay on his bed for the rest of the night. I don't know what he was thinking, but I wondered if he hated Dad as much as I did. And I wondered if Dallas blamed me. I still wonder if he blames me. As much as I wish to eradicate that memory, I also wish I knew whether Dallas blames me or not. I'll never know, but I blame myself and that might be even worse.

As I looked in at Dad, he seemed satisfied. Satisfied: the monster has just unleashed his anger and will on a child who is defenseless against the monster's power. The child yields with painful screams, but does he really learn anything? The purposeful father would explain the wrong and provide an understanding of what is right and appropriate. But this isn't discipline; it is abuse. There is no way to explain the purposefulness of abuse.

Here is a man who seems to think that children were brought into this world to get him his next beer and do yard work. He's married to a compassionate woman so dedicated to her family, faith and values that she can't leave him. She took vows stating she would not. What about his vows? Didn't he also promise "for better or for worse"? Didn't he vow to "accept children lovingly"? She was living her vows while he was providing the "worse". She must have felt trapped in the middle of a trinity, but not the one she had learned in Catholic school. This was a trinity made of the man she thought she married, the values and faith that she had been raised with and the monster who was in front of her.

To take away one's hope and leave them helpless has to be the greatest cruelty of man. I spent much of my childhood curled up in the corner, helpless and hopeless, knowing I could do nothing to stop this. I dreamed of ways to stop it, but never found one.

CHAPTER LESSONS

Physical abuse is not the only form of abuse. It is the one most obvious, but likely the one that heals the fastest.

Emotional and mental abuse attach themselves to every physical abuse. You cannot separate them just as we cannot separate the body from the spirit.

Physical pains often heal without scarring. Emotional abuse scars the brain and the heart. It exists out of sight to others and can exist out of our own awareness for so many years. But the scarring is part of the blackboard that drives us.

The brain and heart need a process to overcome the mental and emotional scars. There was a process that built these scars layer by layer and we all need a process to heal them layer by layer.

ThoughtShredder Moment

As you continue through The Recognition and Rid Phases, keep in mind that not all abuse is physical. Recognize that you might not have been the one being directly abused at all times. Witnessing the abuse and hearing the negative comments about others can have a major impact on you indirectly.

In this chapter, I shared with you my experience watching and hearing the abuse given to another person whom I loved dearly. Not being physically part of this event still had an immense impact on me. There were other moments as well where physical abuse wasn't present, but abuse was still happening. These were the times when my father talked down to me, telling me I was too small, too weak or too lazy. There were comments about how I would never amount to anything and questions about why I could never get anything right. These are limiting, negative comments that a child takes to heart.

You may not have experienced the childhood I had; still, these types of negative comments are everywhere. Listen well enough and you'll hear them on TV, read them in the paper, and find them permeating your work environment. Some people just seem to love being negative and telling you what your limitations are. It's easy for us to get sucked into the conversation and suddenly we believe them and repeat the same comments. When you hear these, remind yourself that they are really talking about their own limitations and don't really know yours.

Use The Recognize and Rid Phases when you hear any negative comments about yourself. Don't limit the process to your childhood memories. Start there, but also bring it into your current life.

ACTION PLAN

Become a great listener. Open up your ears and your mind to all the negative comments that are around you. When you hear one about you, open your journal, write it down and rip it up; rid yourself of it. That other person cannot define who you are. If you hear negative comments being made to others, talk to them. Reaffirm for them that they don't have to believe the other person. A good way to start this is to recognize when you are making negative comments yourself. Write them down and rip them up.

Becoming a great listener will open up a new world for you.

REPLACEMENT THOUGHTS

7

THE BUCKER MOMENT

It's almost noon and lunch needs to be made for the three older kids. I scan the pantry for a box of their favorite meal, macaroni and cheese. There's none available today, so it looks like sandwiches will be the entrée with grapes on the side. I pull out a small colander, fill it with grapes and set it in the sink with the faucet on to wash them.

As I pull the bread out of the pantry, I hear loud thuds moving down the staircase. It's Carson who just found a football in his toyroom. "Look what I found, Dad!" he yells with excitement. "Let's play football." He just wants to play catch and what dad wouldn't?

"I'm making lunch right now. How about after lunch?"

"But, Dad, I want to play now."

The twins will likely be up after lunch, so I agree to play for a few minutes before lunch. Carson curls one arm around the ball and then throws his other fist into the air, jumping and spinning with enthusiasm. He's so excited he trips out the back door, but catches himself and makes it to the middle of the lawn before I can get out of the kitchen.

I laugh out loud as I watch him use his whole body to make the ball go just a few feet. He asks me why I'm laughing and I tell him that he makes me so happy that a smile alone simply won't cover it. I throw the ball over his head and watch him run after it. He picks it up, runs about ten feet closer to me and heaves the ball again. The ball appears to be half the size of his little body, but he doesn't care. As he runs after another errant throw, I suddenly see Scott on the other side of my throws ...

"Throw it here, I'm open!" I shout as I run down the front lawn. Scott steps back and heaves a pass my way, but it's well over my head. Scott is my older brother who is closest in age to me, but physically has a larger build. The age difference and his build allow him to throw much farther than I can. He and I are playing catch on the front lawn, leisurely tossing a football back and forth and discussing world issues: the issues of a world for the typical seven-year-old and nine-year-old.

"Let's pretend we are in the Super Bowl. I'm Kenny Stabler," Scott states.

"I get to be the Cowboys!" I yell back as I run after the errant pass.

Both of us had the Green Bay Packers as our favorite team. We got that from listening to Dad talk about Bart Starr and Vince Lombardi. By the summer of 1972, Vince was gone and Bart was standing on the sidelines as an assistant coach. The better teams were the Dallas Cowboys and the Oakland Raiders. I assume that's why we picked those teams.

"Bob Hays is wide open down the sidelines with five seconds left in the game," I call out, pretending to be one of the *Monday Night Football* crew. "Kenny Stabler moves to his right, sets, and heaves a pass downfield. He's open. It's caught by Hays. He cuts back inside the tackler. Time has expired. One man to beat and he busts through the tackle, dives into the end zone, and the Cowboys win. Bob Hays has just won the Super Bowl for the Dallas Cowboys!" I spike the ball and jump up and down with my arms raised, scanning the imaginary crowd.

Now it's Scott's turn to be Fred Biletnikoff catching a pass from Roger Staubach. Scott goes for the flare of a diving, circus catch in the end zone for his turn. We continue this for much of the early afternoon that Saturday.

Isn't it interesting how a child's mind works? I was "wide open" but still managed to weave around defenders and break tackles. Not to mention that the quarterbacks we pretended to be were on opposite teams as the receivers they were throwing to. That's the world of a kid—I couldn't pretend to be a member of Scott's favorite team, no way. In a kid's world, things don't always have to make sense, and yet the important things, family things do have to make sense. Things like: a dad having innate love for a son and showing it. Things like: why do we get punishment one day for the same acts that were all right a different day? There seem to be different levels to a child's mind, each needing a different degree of understanding. Maybe it's the difference between the real world and our pretend world.

The time we had on the front lawn was playtime for us, but also escape-time.

Back on the front lawn, Scott and I have won the Super Bowl countless times with various imaginary plays. We're getting tired, so Scott tucks the ball under his arm and sits on the ground. Pulling the wide blades of grass out, we try to make our version of bird calls with the grass between our thumbs. More talk about worldly events ensues as we lay on the grass watching the clouds. We talk about our dreams of growing up.

Scott wants to be a football player. He'd like to play for the Green Bay Packers, but will settle for the Oakland Raiders.

I also have dreams of being a football player, but not today. Today, I tell Scott about my other dreams of growing up. "I want to grow up and join the Army so I can learn karate then come back and beat up Dad." Scott has other dreams too, but he's not shocked in the least by mine. We both agree that it will be 100 years before we are grown up, and then go back to playing football.

I'm a seven-year-old kid who wants to play football and pretend to be James Kirk flying around the galaxy. While my friends dream of being a professional football or basketball player, a fireman or doctor, I dream of beating up my dad. I'm tired of the abuse. I'm tired of the anger and I want him to feel the pain he is inflicting on us. I want him to hurt so I can say, "There, how does that feel? You don't like it much, do you? Now stop doing it to us."

I just know in my heart that if he feels it, he'll understand and stop. Isn't that why he hits us, so we can learn to stop and do the right thing? So often I wonder what that right thing is.

It's my first Bucker moment. It's the biggest moment and will create the wedge between my dad and I; I need to be a different person. It's the moment that my brain started the concept of re-programming. I didn't realize it then, but it has become evident to me since I started my journey.

I never got the chance to fulfill that dream, but I'm not sure if the desire ever really diminished. I still work out on heavy weights to this day. I enjoy the characteristic of having physical power. I took on my dad's frame and got some of his strength. Being a small man, I have always been able to lift significant amounts of weight without a lot of training. Even into my 40's, I continue to lift for power. I wonder, am I still waiting to beat up Dad?

CHAPTER LESSONS

Bucker moments are times when you consciously choose to be different than your programming.

I was a victim of this violence, but the violence is now done. I will only remain a victim as long as I allow the mental and emotional effects to remain.

Dad can't hurt me in the physical sense anymore, and he can't hurt me in the mental and emotional senses either, as long as I don't let him.

Many don't know the affects until they have passed. Once we understand them, we can move forward ensuring they don't hurt us again.

ThoughtShredder Moment

PHASE THREE:
THE REPLACEMENT PHASE

Moving forward is the greatest feeling for a Bucker. To this point, I have asked you to continuously go into your past and relive the events, write them down, then rid yourself of them by ripping them up. These are essential phases in the process in order to set the landscape of your life with a new foundation. However, that house we discussed in an earlier example isn't going to last long on a new foundation if we don't start building it.

The next phase of ThoughtShredder is Replacement. It's time to start building the foundation of new beliefs within you. At this point, many of you will be saying, "Wait, I don't want to completely change who I am. I like who I am." That's great. You should like who you are. But all of us have more within us to achieve.

In this phase I'm not asking you to change everything about you; I'm asking you to start building the new beliefs from those you have ripped away. This is one of the most fun parts of the whole process. It's like having a blank canvas in front of you with no writer's block. Pretend you have a blank check for the future and you can write any amount on it to get and be anything you want. The best part is that this is in your mind and heart, so no one can foreclose on your thoughts. Sit back and dream a bit.

As you begin this phase, continue to remind yourself that there are no limits. When you limit yourself in thinking, you are using someone else's thoughts or actions from the past against yourself. That's what the first two phases were all about. When you begin limiting yourself with thoughts that you can't do something, go back to the beginning of the process. Recognize the thought and rid yourself of it. Now go back to dreaming.

Don't be surprised or disappointed when those limiting thoughts come back. They'll continue to be there for awhile. Remember, it took many years to build on them. It's going to take some time to rid you of them. The final phase of ThoughtShredder works on that.

ACTION PLAN

Start dreaming, you deserve it. Start thinking about and picturing in your mind all that you want to have and accomplish. Write these down in your journal. Next to these write down the emotions these will bring to you. Go back to your journal often and remind yourself of all that you want and deserve. Build some hope inside of yourself.

We can shape the future; start acting now to shape it.

Replacement Thoughts

8

GROWN UP SPANKING

Lunch is served. I'm done playing football with Carson and the kids are eating turkey sandwiches, each with a slightly different twist. Lauren likes mayo and lettuce, but no cheese. Carson likes mayo and cheese, but no lettuce. Megan likes all of it.

Each of them takes their plate to the kitchen table to sit and eat. Now it's time to take turns at getting a juice box or cup of water. They are finally seated. Each of them position themselves on the side of the table closest to the kitchen area so they can face the living room with a perfect view of the TV.

"Can we watch TV?"

I click the remote and find one of their favorite channels. Sponge-Bob is on doing crazy things and talking in his crazy voice. The kids love it, but I'm less than thrilled.

I shake my head and wonder what happened to the good old cartoons like *The Scooby-Doo Show* and *Jonny Quest*? For that matter, what happened to all the good shows that used to entertain me as a child? I'm sure my parents thought the same thing about the TV shows they watched and the music they listened to …

"No you can't leave me, you can't!" came the unmistakable fake cry from Carol Burnett. As we watched in laughter, Carol was playing a character whose husband was leaving her. Harvey Korman was playing the husband role. Dressed in a leisure suit and heading for the front door, Korman's character was slowed by Burnett. She was holding onto his lower leg as he continued to move toward the door, dragging her along.

The whole audience was laughing as were we. It seemed anything Carol Burnett did was funny, even if she made fun of a serious event, and even if we didn't really know what divorce meant at the time.

Scott got up from our seated position on the floor in front of the TV. He began walking to the kitchen for something when I grabbed his leg and wrapped my arms around it. "Don't leave," I joked. "Don't divorce me."

Scott quickly picked up on the game and played along dragging me for a few steps. I continued my pleas, trying my best to sound like Carol Burnett.

"Cut that out," came the stern voice of Dad. "We don't talk about divorce in this family."

As with most incidents, I didn't know why I was stopping. I knew I didn't want the possible retribution, so we stopped. Dad looked not so much angry, but upset. With his angry reactions, I would have cowered expecting a slap. I had no sense that he was about to hit anyone. His voice seemed more nervous or scared than angry.

I still wasn't really sure what divorce meant, but I certainly had the impression that Mom had talked to Dad about something. Whatever divorce meant, it was the only thing I had known that scared Dad. Not long after that incident, his fears were realized.

I don't remember the police car coming down the road or turning into our driveway; I just remember it being there. Most of the scenes from that day are broken into pieces within my memory. It was a summer day and I think it was sunny, but I can't be sure. A policeman handed Dad some papers while Mom was at work. I was playing somewhere else and didn't see the actual delivery. I was told this later. I had a sense that something wasn't right, but I really didn't know what this all meant.

As we walked into the kitchen, there was Dad, tears in his eyes, holding the papers. He looked toward us, but not at us. He shook the papers and asked us why Mom would do this. It was a weird feeling. I figured that it meant Dad had to leave. If I was right, why was he asking that question? Wasn't it obvious? Weren't you here all this time? How long did you expect her to take this? The reasons why seemed pretty clear to me. Where had he been?

How could someone be so blind to his own faults? Still, part of me felt sorry for Dad. He was crying for the first time that I could remember. And now that I am older and have experienced loss, I can imagine how his heart was tearing up. The sense of loss and loneliness must have been devastating. He was only seven when his dad died. This must have seemed as crushing. I hated to see anyone in pain and yet I wanted out of this kind of life, his kind of life.

I stood there watching him while battling my emotions of, "Yes, I want you to leave," and "No, I don't want you to be hurt." It was as if I couldn't get both to live in the same mind. Now that I can recall my feelings, I wonder if this is also how Mom felt. Was she struggling with her emotions and holding back from acting sooner?

My brothers and I went down to the bridge to play and lose track of our thoughts the rest of the day. We left Dad at home where I imagine he got ready and reluctantly left for work.

Down by the bridge, we met my cousin, Mark. In our conversations with him, I began to realize that whatever was going on, Dallas was very upset about it. Mark could sense it too, but he knew even less than I did. Mark tried to joke with Dallas at first, but Dallas was not in the mood. Dallas had told us as we walked down to the bridge that we shouldn't tell anyone about this. "Why not," I wondered? "It's not like Dad's gone forever. Mom just made sure he couldn't hurt us anymore." That's the way I took it and if I'm right, what's wrong with that?

Finally Dallas spilled the beans to Mark. Dallas had tears coming down his cheeks as he told him. Suddenly, I felt bad too, but I didn't know why.

We played at the bridge for an hour or so, but Dallas seemed to be thinking more than playing. I threw stones in the water, pretending I was trying to skip them across the surface. Pretending meant that I was really throwing them straight down and hoping that someone would recognize that I was upset. It was my way of trying to show everyone that I knew what was going on, but I really didn't. If Dallas is upset, then I must be too even though I didn't feel it. I just knew my brother was and I wanted to be like him.

Why was Dallas so upset about this? Dad treated him worse than me and I was glad. I thought I was glad. "Isn't this what I wanted? Isn't this what we all wanted?"

Dallas wanted to stay down by the bridge the rest of the day. Had he had his preference, I think he would have packed a suitcase, set up the tent and lived there away from the shame of his parents getting a divorce.

He knew we had to go back eventually and after awhile, he realized that staying here into the night still wouldn't have the direct impact he wanted. He wanted to show Mom that we didn't approve of this. "Let's go back home," he called, gathering us all in a group. He wanted her to know that he had learned from her— stay strong; put up a good front; don't let others know the family secret. Isn't that what she had been doing? She can't just change the rules now. You've taught us a style and we are living it out.

We walked back to the house not saying much, but the wheels were turning in Dallas' head. He was working on a plan for us to show Mom how we felt. We arrived back at the house about thirty minutes before Mom was to get home. I went to turn on the TV, but Dallas stopped me. He had a plan and was ready to share it.

"We're going to sit in the bedroom and do nothing, say nothing. When Mom comes home, don't talk to her. We're going to sit here in this room."

"Okay," I thought. "Dallas knows more than I do about what's going on. He's the guy I look up to. He's the guy I want to grow up to be. I'm going to do what he does. This should be pretty cool. I'm involved and part of a plan."

Mom walked into the house seemingly like any other afternoon, but I imagine she felt quite different. At some level, there must have been comfort and peace, knowing her ordeals with his brutality were over. Another side of her must have been wondering what she would do alone, living in the country with no one around for half a mile or so. For me, as a kid, the distance seemed more like ten miles; I imagine that day it felt the same to her. Sure, she had us kids to keep her company at night, but another part of her life, her view of what life was supposed to be like, was torn away. As a little girl, I'm sure she didn't dream of her marriage being like this, nor ending like this.

I sat in that bedroom when Mom came home playing the game Dallas had put us up to. Mom called for us, but we didn't answer. That was the plan. I could hear footsteps moving her around the house, searching. She stopped at the bottom of the stairs looking up and calling for us, but no answer. She walked down the hall to the bedroom and opened the door. There we were, sitting quietly, looking down, and ignoring her. I glanced up at her ready to hug her like I normally did, but then looked at Dallas who had his back to her and I looked back down. "Remember the plan," I thought. Then Mom spoke and I could no longer play along.

"So this is how it's going to be. You're punishing me for leaving your father."

I could hear the pain in Mom's voice. Her eyes began to tear up, but no real tears would come. She was too tough for that. But I could hear the pain and the internal turmoil she was going through. Her fears all day, knowing that Dad was getting his notice this morning, had to be about him actually leaving. Would he be gone as directed by the sheriff or would he still be there, waiting for her to explain this? Was this really over or did she just make it worse? Those questions had to be running through her head as she made the trip home.

As she drove into the driveway just moments ago and saw that his car was gone, she must have felt some relief and some pride knowing she had finally taken the right step. She might have to deal with him again later, but for now he was gone. Life was going to be a lot different with him gone, but at least she still had her children. What a surprise to find that her children had turned on her.

"Did your dad put you up to this?" she questioned.

"No," was the succinct response, and she walked out of the bedroom to the kitchen showing that incredible pain on her face.

It was over for me. This was supposed to be a game: a bonding between Dallas and me. I was showing him that I was with him and being with him, he had to be with me. If I showed him my support, he wouldn't leave too. But now, this had gone too far. Mom didn't deserve this.

Before she got to the kitchen, I was on her waist. I caught her from behind and hugged her. She reached back and pressed me harder against her. Now some tears came. She asked, "Did you want me to leave your father?"

"Yes," was my succinct response.

For Dallas, living with the physical abuse and emotional pain of the violence was more desirable, more tolerable than the shame and guilt of others knowing his parents were getting a divorce. The mind can be a crazy apparatus. How powerful shame can be. Thank God Mom overcame her feelings of shame and made the brave choice.

For the first time, I began to understand; at least I thought I did. I saw that this was not an easy decision for her. I didn't know why it was hard, but I knew that it was. Still, I didn't get it all. I thought this was like giving Dad a spanking. As we were spanked and were supposed to learn to do the right thing, he too would feel the pain and learn to do the right thing. Isn't that what spankings are about? Isn't that the purpose of punishment? Did he know this was a spanking? And did he know what the right thing was? I had all these questions and no answers. I would never get my answers directly from him, but the choices he made became loud, clear answers for me.

I didn't know that he would soon be gone and out of my life almost completely. And the even more surprising part was that it was his choice.

People wonder why a victim of abuse stays, but now I can see partly why. The emotional battle with shame and guilt is tough. Change is hard and the uncertain future, scary.

Over the next few years, Dad made poor decision after poor decision. At the time, his actions really confused me. I knew that he was a smart person, the smartest I had known. Whenever I had a question, he seemed to know the answer, about everything. He knew about science. He knew about biology. He knew math. He knew construction. If I had a question about the weather, he could explain why it was happening. I don't recall a time that I stumped him on any subject. I remember thinking he was a mean person, but, wow, what a smart person too. But for some reason, he couldn't control his anger; he couldn't stop drinking and he couldn't get the break he needed to make it successfully. He tried other jobs, but couldn't hold them. He tried managing a bar, but lost it. The smartest guy I knew couldn't figure out his own life. And things were about to get worse for him.

CHAPTER LESSONS

The blackboards of our lives also carry great lessons. It's important to look back on them and learn from them.

Mom showed me the first sign of being a Bucker. She wasn't going to settle for what she had. There were too many others being affected. She was brave and committed. Learn from the Buckers in your life.

Avoiding shame can be an incredible motivator. We covered these acts up for a long time. What are you covering up about yourself? You don't need to tell everyone, but admit it to yourself and to those whom you want to grow with.

Those in the family of the abuser can learn controlling mechanisms like shame and guilt. Learn to recognize them and buck the opportunity to use them on others.

Don't judge; just accept that the people you meet have childhood experiences different from your own. Each of our experiences in childhood develops the blackboard inside of us.

ThoughtShredder Moment

Becoming a Chaos Kid requires having role models who were chaotic. We grow up watching how the major influencers in our lives act and we naturally take on their actions. How many times have you said to yourself, "Oh my God, that's just what my mother/father used to say,"?

Being a Bucker is no different. We are helped by having a role model who is a Bucker. During a time when her family, her community and her religion frowned upon divorce, my mother bucked them all. She made the decision to kick my father out and, more importantly, she followed through with action. My mother didn't just dream of a new life, she made it happen.

There was pain involved in that decision and the actions that followed. There was doubt, frustration, fear and anxiety. She prevailed knowing there was a greater good to be done; a larger impact to be made on her children.

Are you feeling any of those emotions now? Are you doubting yourself because of fear? It's natural. Don't use that as an excuse to give up. Keep pushing through. The new you, the real you, will be so grateful for it.

ACTION PLAN

Now that you have a list of dreams of what you want to have and want to accomplish, you might be wondering how in the world you're going to go about fulfilling those dreams. Start by finding a role model who has accomplished what you want to accomplish. Have coffee or lunch with him or her. Tell them how much you respect what they have done with their life. Ask them how they did it. At times you'll be amazed at how easy it is and at times you'll doubt yourself. During the doubts, pull out your journal. You know what to do.

Don't allow the shame and guilt brought on by someone else to continue to drive you. Take control.

REPLACEMENT THOUGHTS

9

SYMPTOMS VERSUS CAUSE

The girls want to play on the trampoline since the twins are sleeping again. "Can you jump with us, Dad, please?" they beg.

Without a verbal answer, I slowly get off the couch and then run to back door to get on the trampoline first. Megan and Lauren run after me shouting, "Hey, that isn't fair!"

Carson is sleeping too, so it's just us three bouncing around. Megan jumps off to get some balls for us to kick while we jump. She tosses a few over the screen that surrounds the trampoline and keeps us securely on the black, bouncy surface. She carries the last two with her as she climbs back on.

"Let's play You Can't Touch a Ball," demands Megan. It's a fun game that provides a much needed exercise break for me, even though I always lose. After each game, we flop down on the trampoline and rejuvenate our drained bodies. It's amazing how tired I am after the game, but I don't think about it at all while playing. This is what it feels like to be a kid again.

Carson's awake and headed out the back door to join us. "I never win at this game," I state. "Let's do butt bombs instead."

Everyone agrees as we let Carson on. Each of us gets a turn to do a trick that ends with a butt bomb: jumping up and landing smack on your butt. The girls are doing half flips, twirls and handstands. Carson is too young to do those so he spins around and throws in a few summersaults. He's not happy though. He really wants to do the flips.

Within a few minutes Carson is sitting on the side of the trampoline, arms folded and head down. He's mad about something. I crawl over to him and put my arm around him. He shoves me away. He's one of the sweetest kids I know and wouldn't hurt anyone, but he has a temper. I don't like tempers.

"What's wrong now?" I question.

"Nothing!" is his response. He's stubborn too.

"Did you get hurt?" I question further.

"No."

"Then what's wrong?"

"It was my turn," he finally admits.

Parenting 101 kicks in. "Is this how you show us what's wrong? What do you do if you have a problem?" I often make the mistake of assuming my children have fully developed, reasoning brains.

"Okay, Carson. It's your turn!" Lauren shouts.

Out from under my arm Carson bounces with a big smile on his face. "Watch this," he states as he begins his twisting stunt again. He's completely recovered without any help from me and my sage parenting.

Carson spins so wildly that he accidently flips to a handstand and over onto his back. "Wow, did you see that, Dad?" his wide eyes show the excitement of accomplishing his first flip. "Did you see that? I did a flip."

I'm about to engage my logical adult brain and tell him that's not really a flip, that's more of a handspring. A flip is when you ... but I remember how that parenting style didn't work just two minutes ago. Instead, I just say, "Yes, you're a big man now."

The words aren't even out of my mouth before the scene starts playing in my head. It amazes me how quickly memories can engage.

"How do I look?" Mom asked as she walked into the kitchen. That familiar cracking sound coming from her gum and a mixture of mint and perfume scents following right behind. We all agree that she looks great.

Mom seemed to take forever to get ready for that date, but wow, did she ever look pretty. For many of my younger years, I thought my mom was the prettiest person in the world. With little money to work with, she always found ways to look stylish and pretty. She had jumpsuits with flared pants, dresses with simple sweaters and plain old jeans, but they all looked good on her. Since the divorce though, she hadn't had too many chances to dress up and look like that woman again. Tonight, that lady was back.

Mom waited awhile before she started dating again. She had so much to do with taking care of us and making sure the house payments were made—something Dad didn't help with very often. Still, she needed more in her life, more than what us kids could provide. She was a young woman and needed companionship. I was searching for a grown man who would listen to me and hug me. I assumed she needed the same.

I followed her around the house as she continued to get ready. It seemed like a new and fun experience for me also. Mom kept asking me if I was okay with her going out with someone. Now that I can look back, I wonder if she was asking me or asking herself.

I thought it was great. Why wouldn't I? Isn't this all a part of Dad's spanking? You'll do this for a while until Dad gets the help he needs and comes back having learned his lesson. That's the way I looked at it, but I never told her that. I just assumed she knew.

She left the house looking great, but still acting nervous. Was she nervous about the date or nervous about something else? What could possibly go wrong on a first date? Early in the morning, I was sleeping in my bed, still with Scott, but without the bunks. We quickly heard what could go wrong.

The opening of the front door woke me up from a very restless sleep. I was excited for Mom and wanted to stay up until she got home, but I couldn't last. Now she was home again and I felt excited to run down the steps and see her.

Mom was getting the man a drink, but I got the sense that she was ready for the date to be over. My excitement began to turn to anxiety. I wanted to run down and hug her, but he was still there and I felt uncomfortable with him. It was my first experience with feeling intimidated by a man other than my father. I didn't know this man at all, but for some reason he made me nervous.

Mom must have seen the lights of another car out the kitchen window. The driveway was some two hundred yards long with a bend in it about fifty yards from the house. Any car coming down the driveway at night couldn't avoid having the headlights flash through the kitchen window. As kids, we used that sign to know that Mom and Dad were home and it was time to quickly clean up whatever we had done. Tonight, Mom was already home and Dad was about to be.

"Someone's here," Mom said with some surprise and a little bit of expectedness. "Oh God, it's Dallas," she continued as she ran to the front door. She locked the door with the deadbolt before Dad could get to it. Dad must have been running because he got to the door just after she locked it. He pounded on the door and yelled at those inside to let him in, but there was no way Mom was doing that. She pleaded for him to leave, but there was no way he was doing that. The pounding became much heavier as Dad began putting his shoulder into the door. Nothing it seemed was going to hold him out.

"Let him in," Mom's date told her, Dad still pounding on door.

"I'm not going to let him in."

"Then let him break the door down, I don't care," came his uncaring response. At this point, he seemed much more interested in confronting Dad than in his date.

"Who's going to pay for the door," Mom questioned?

"You," came the again uncompassionate response.

Dad yelled some words through the door that I couldn't understand, but the response from Mom's date stuck with me. "I've handled bigger and better men than you before." How arrogant he seemed now. My uncomfortable feeling about him was being confirmed. On the other hand, here was a chance for Dad to be shown the pain that he had inflicted on us. I didn't want anyone to be hurt and I despised fighting, but maybe Dad could learn something from this. Maybe this could be another spanking for Dad.

Dad came through the door with a loud crash. In my bed, the familiar tantrum began again. I plugged my ears and yelled out loud attempting to drown out the sounds. "Please, don't let me hear this again," I thought to myself. But as hard as I tried, I couldn't avoid hearing some of it. There were groans and a lot of banging sounds as I imagine the two grown men wrestled around the kitchen and dining room. Within moments it was over, no more sounds. We all ran down the steps to see Dad getting off the other guy, he reaching for his knee in pain. Dad had won the battle, but lost so much.

As his four boys looked on, he looked over at us, breathing heavy from the scuffle. Dallas looked right at him and said, "I suppose you think you're a big man now."

It was as if he too wanted Dad to lose, just this one time. He stood bravely continuing to look at Dad as he walked by. Dad slapped

Dallas on the chest almost in desperation. It seemed he didn't really know how to respond. He looked spent, dejected, and at a loss for words. He said nothing, but the look on his face told me so much. The rejection from his son took its toll as he stumbled out the door.

How crushing that must have felt for Dad. As much as I hated Dad for being there and doing what he did, on another level I felt sorry for him again. Had he just walked out and we said nothing, I would have just been angry and frustrated that this man can never leave peacefully. But Dallas had to make that comment, an arrow to any other man's heart, and to mine. I can't imagine Dad not feeling it too. His face reflected back the feelings in his heart. He had lost his wife to another man and his children had turned on him too.

Now I was really confused. How can I hate a man and feel sorry for him at the same time? And I had so many more questions about Dad. Why did he think beating someone else up would make Mom come back to him? Why would she be impressed with that? What was he thinking? I was confused between the pain I felt *for* him and the pain I felt *from* him.

I wanted to run after him and tell him he missed his chance for a spanking. "This was all supposed to be for your own good. This is how you treat us sometimes. You're our father. Please come back and learn to treat us like your children." But even that pleading from a young boy in a white t-shirt would likely disappear into the black night.

The front door slammed shut and the last we heard from Dad for a while was the sound of a revving engine and tires spinning wildly in the gravel.

Nothing was the same from that point on. I think I began to realize that this wasn't a spanking for Dad. If it was meant to be, he wasn't learning. Dad wasn't coming back into the family, but he was still around. His relationship with Mom was irreconcilable, but maybe his relationship with me could be changed. Maybe we could get to a true father-son relationship like I had imagined, like my friends seemed to have.

Not long after that, Dad left for Arizona and never came back again. Physically, he visited Wisconsin a few times, but Dad, the Dad I wanted, never came home. To be honest, I don't know if he was ever really there.

I was thirteen years old and wouldn't see my dad again for ten years. In all those years he missed so much. He never watched me play a single game of football and only watched my wrestling in grade school. I don't know if he ever knew about the pole vaulting or my college graduation. He met my first daughter when she was one, but never met the rest of my children. He knew I was married, but never attended the ceremony or sent a card. He met my wife only once during the funeral of his younger brother. She saw him one other time as he laid in his coffin in the funeral home.

Dad, didn't you know that loving me meant providing for me at all times? It meant supporting me? It meant being there when I had my proudest moments, even if the accomplishments were way less than you expected? Didn't you know that moving away meant abandonment and left me wondering whom I would turn to for advice and support? Didn't you know that a father's love is unconditional? Don't you remember your father's love?

All of these questions spun in my mind waiting to ask him directly, but then, as with so many other things in life, it was too late.

During those childhood years, no bones were broken, that I know of, and no one was hospitalized or worse. Maybe I should consider myself lucky to have survived the physical pain and my brothers and sister with me. Maybe these memories should all be swept under the rug and marked down as good lessons. Others have endured so much worse. Shouldn't I feel lucky? Isn't that exactly what I have been doing since that first incident as a five-year-old boy, sweeping them under the rug? How much has that helped me since?

After Dad left, I assumed all the pain would end and all the scars would heal. This part of my life would be over and I would have the chance to live "normally" from now on. I was about to realize the difference between physical and emotional abuse. I was about to learn how debilitating the long-term effects can be. Even though Dad was gone, I couldn't just wash him out of my mind. The program had been set. When would it kick in and how would I reprogram it?

CHAPTER LESSONS

Getting rid of the symptoms doesn't get rid of the problem. Getting rid of the source doesn't get rid of the effects. Getting Dad out of the house didn't remove all the memories.

Everyone has a blackboard. Dad had problems of his own. Removing him from the home did not cure his abusive behavior. He learned it somewhere and needed to unlearn it.

Programming is strong; if a person is to change, they first have to have desire to change.

We don't own each other. People are not property. We are here to influence others, not to control them.

ThoughtShredder Moment

Remember, everyone has a blackboard. Everyone has issues: some are greater than yours and yours are greater than some, but we all have them. We can choose to allow these issues to rule us and run our lives without knowing it. We can avoid the conscious realization that these events happened. We can continue moving on with our lives allowing the scars to exist, allowing the words and actions of others to keep us in fear of being who we can be.

Recognize the past, and then recognize that the past is just that, the past. It is gone and cannot be changed. The people who hurt us in the past cannot continue to do so if we don't let them. Doesn't it seem a bit crazy when you think about how someone who is out of our lives, maybe even gone from this world, can still affect us so dramatically?

One way that we continue to let the past rule us is with the present. What I mean is that my father continued to show up in my life even though he was gone. A comment or even a simple gesture by someone in my life would bring me back to memories of my dad and how he handled the situation. If a voice was raised, I waited for someone to be hit. I wasn't back in my childhood, but I was bringing my childhood into my present moment. The circumstances were completely different, but I put them together in my mind and heart and let them control me.

Action Plan

It's time to get specific. Continue to recognize the past, but begin relating it to the present. Understand how you are allowing others to affect you because of past events. Write these down. Review them and rid yourself of them. Then write down how you will feel and act differently in the future. Write down what is really happening. I would write down, "This man is not my father. He is not going to hurt me. He just has a different opinion and is passionate about it. A raised voice does not mean physical pain."

The new you is coming out and making a difference. Do you feel it?

REPLACEMENT THOUGHTS

10

BEFORE IT'S TOO LATE

Clouds filled the sky on this warm June day, but I could see a line of blue sky well to the south. That's where I was headed with the minivan packed with dirty clothes, beddings, leftover food and three young kids. It was another great weekend at the cottage.

"Twenty minutes to home!" I shouted to the back of the van. No response. Everyone was sleeping. Lauren moved a bit, but settled herself and fell back into dreamland.

I picked up my phone to check for messages. "What's wrong?" asked Tracy, noticing the puzzled look on my face.

"I have two messages and a bunch of missed calls. I wonder what that's all about." I put my phone back down assuming these were business related and I would get to them after we got home and unpacked the van.

As we reached the edge of town my curiosity got the best of me. I picked up my voicemails and had a few from my brother Scott. He left no indication of the news, just stated that he was trying to get a hold of me and that I should call him or Mom as soon as I could. My first concern was for Mom, but if I was to call her, she must be okay.

We pulled into the garage and unpacked—as was normal with every other weekend we'd spent up there. As we walked into the house, we could hear the beeping of our answering machine. Six messages were left, not completely unusual for a weekend away, but most of the people who call us regularly were with us at the cabin. Now this seemed odd.

As we listened to each message I could sense something wasn't right. The messages were from Scott and my mom asking me to call them back. They had started on Saturday morning and it was now Sunday afternoon around 4:00 p.m. Each message seemed to be more pleading. "Please call us back as soon as you can," was the end of each.

The fifth message finally broke the news. It was from my mother who had left other messages without indication of the news. This time she noted that this was not something she should leave in a voicemail, but since they can't get a hold of me, she had to tell me. "There's no other way to say this except, your father died yesterday morning."

My wife fell back against the cupboard holding her hand over her mouth in much more shock than I was. Removing her hand, she said, "Oh my God, I was just thinking that on the way home. I was thinking, 'If your dad dies, what would we do? He's in Arizona. Would we go there or have him buried up here? Would the kids come with us? Who do we know in Arizona?'"

I had the same question, "What will we do?" But mine was less about the logistics of events. It was more about what will I do, how will I feel, and how will I react?

Tracy felt a little guilty for a moment, imagining someone's death before it happened. She felt sad knowing that my father was gone and was likely putting herself in my shoes, as she so aptly does. She felt for me. I felt nothing, nothing I could explain or could have anticipated. I had feelings, but I wasn't sure what they were.

I hugged my wife in an attempt to console myself, but it didn't work. It wasn't that holding her wasn't comforting; it was very comforting. The problem was that I didn't feel a need to be comforted. Dad was gone and I felt myself searching my mind and heart for the emotions I thought should be there, but they didn't exist. They may have existed somewhere, but I couldn't find them. Shouldn't they just pour out of me?

Dad had not taken care of himself much; he didn't eat particularly healthfully nor did he exercise. After spending most of his adult life drinking heavily, I was told that he had pretty much quit that during the last few years; still, health wasn't a top priority for him. His death wasn't as much of a shock as was the thought that he lived so long with his lifestyle. Still, the lack of shock was not the reason I felt no need for comfort.

As I spoke with family members, I learned more about Dad's last days. That week, he had been in the hospital for surgery to remove his leg from just below the knee. He had suffered from blood clots for many years and recently, one had lodged in his leg cutting off vital circulation and causing significant pain. Doctors recommended the surgery to avoid the risk of the clot dislodging and doing more damage in his heart or brain. Even though the surgery went well and Dad was in good spirits afterwards, a few days after the surgery, apparently, that is exactly what happened with a different clot. It released from some other part of his body and caused a massive heart attack.

Now he was gone. I would see him no more, speak to him no more, and touch him no more. But wait, I hadn't spoken to him in about five years, not since his younger brother died of a similar heart attack. Before that, I don't even remember the last time I saw him or spoke to him. I thought about him. I invited him to my wedding. I went to visit him. I even wrote him a letter once just after I graduated college. With all my attempts, for some fifteen years, each being neglected by him, I moved through my life as though he didn't exist. It was as if he had died many years earlier.

I went downstairs and pulled out a copy of my letter to him. The letter was an attempt to reconcile and connect with him again. I referenced the movie *Field of Dreams*, noting how the son and father left each other in anger. The next time Kevin Costner's character saw his father, it was at his father's funeral. Now, with his field built, his dad was coming back to "ease his pain". I saw the movie in college and immediately wrote the letter.

I wrote about how that made me realize that family members need to reconcile before it's too late. I wrote about how I often dreamed about him being at the doors of the gym or walking onto the field as I finished the biggest match or game of my life. I wrote about getting back together and not letting loss, anger and misunderstanding stand between us. It was time to reconcile and I was willing to start it. No response ever came from him. No acknowledgement of receiving it. No attempt to reconcile. Was I that much of a disappointment to him? As I read that letter again, I began to see the dream I held in my heart for so many years—the dream of Dad being there. I was looking for the *Field of Dreams* ending, but it never came.

My dream started on a wrestling mat. It was the one connection I seemed to have with Dad. He qualified for the state tournament as a senior in high school. My dream began with reality and morphed into fantasy.

In high school, I qualified for the state championship wrestling tournament as a junior. I had a record of twenty wins and two losses going into the regional tournament. I was the top seed in that tournament and made it through, winning each match fairly easily. Next was the sectional tournament. If I finished first or second I'd be going to state. This wouldn't be nearly as easy. Now based on my record, I was the fourth seed.

I won my first match with little trouble, but then came the match against the top-rated wrestler in the tournament. He had previously wrestled and beaten one of my teammates who assured me this would be tough. He was right. It was a grueling match that came down to the last seconds and I ended up short. I needed that victory to get into the championship match and assure myself of a birth at state, or so I thought.

These tournaments were different. They had something called a wrestle-back. If you lose in the second round and that opponent ends up winning the tournament, you can get a chance to wrestle again for second place. So there I sat, having to win my consolation match to be in third place. Then I'd have to root for the guy who beat me in the championship match. If he won then the second place wrestler and I would need to fight it out for the true second place winner. The premise is that they want to reduce the affect of seeding.

I got my wish and was set for a wrestle-back match. It would be my fourth match of the day. Was I ready; was I conditioned for this match? Here was an opportunity to buck before I knew what bucking was. My dad had shown me so many times where he didn't follow through. "We're going to have this," he'd state about a pool or a car or a trip somewhere. But it never seemed to come true. He seemed to have a lack of will to take actions against what his dreams were. I wasn't going to let that happen to me, not this time.

I stepped on that mat with one focus: win. I was ahead in score for most of the match although only by a point or two. Toward the end of the last period, we found ourselves out of bounds on the mat and had to restart. I was up by two and held the top position. All I had to do was maintain control of my opponent for twenty more seconds. But I knew myself better than that. My weakness was holding opponents down. My strength was taking them down. Against my coaches' instructions, I let the other wrestler go as the whistle sounded to start the match again. I let him up, sacrificing a point. Now I held a one-point lead. All he had to do was take me down to the mat and the match would be over, along with my dream of qualifying for state.

My coaches urged me to stall. "Stay away from him! Don't let him get you down!" they kept yelling. Again, that wasn't my style. I want control. As my opponent assumed I would stall and he would have to be the aggressor, I turned the tables on him. I charged in when he expected me to stay back. I grabbed one leg, used a single-leg technique and took him down. I held on for just a few seconds and then felt the incredible relief of the horn. The match was over, the scoreboard showed 12-9 in my favor. The referee raised my hand as the rest of my team mobbed me. I was going to state and my dream would continue.

Dreams, I have found are different than goals. Goals you can control. You can work with incredible determination and will to reach that goal. Dreams are less controllable. They seem more fanciful to me and less tangible, less attainable. My dream started with a birth in the state tournament: a goal achieved. The dream ended with reconciliation with Dad: fantasy. I had control of the first part of that dream, but no control over the second part.

The party after the sectional tournament was amazing. I don't recall whose house we were at, nor do I remember many of the guests. I remember that I just wanted to sit by the fireplace in the basement of this house as my friends ran around yelling, dancing and partying. I just wanted to sit back quietly and soak this in. I wanted to dream.

I pictured myself at the state tournament with all of the fans cheering and stomping their feet on the bleachers. The field house would be alive with energy. The screaming fans would be so loud all you could hear was a roar, no words could be distinguished.

There I was on the center mat in my championship bout. The match would be a struggle of wills, two opponents battling exhaustion, and fighting for their goals. In the end, I would end up the victor. How the match was won was not my concern. My dream was much more about the celebration.

As my hand would be raised in victory as champion, he would be there on the other side of the gym. Our eyes would meet. He'd give me a nod of approval and just the hint of a smile, like he used to do when he looked at the work he had accomplished when I was a child.

I could see him there with his coat on, his hands in his pockets as though he had just gotten off the plane, made no other stops and rushed to the gym just in time for my match. I'd shake my coaches' hands; get hugs and high-fives from my teammates, all the while keeping an eye across the gym as if the image would fade if I glanced away.

I'd make my way around the mats with the action of other matches moving around me: them in slow motion, me in my own world. I would be unfazed by neither the movement on the mats nor the screams and cheers from other fans. I'd get to Dad as he opened his arms and in one movement I would be hugged and picked up off the ground by him. He'd say, "Good job, son. Good job." And I'd know he was proud of me. That was all I needed: Dad with a sense of pride in me.

I had no vision of rekindling anything beyond that. What I wanted most, what I needed most, was just one chance for him to see who I was and what I had become in the five years since he left. He had to see that I was no longer one of "the little ones". I was an athlete, the best athlete. I had accomplished something that he could not do, nor anyone else in my family. This was all about my triumph and my recognition. That was my dream, but dreams don't always come true.

In my real life, I lost the match at state. Intimidated by the surroundings of that huge gym and the thousands of people in it, I let myself lose to an inferior opponent; one whom I later beat. But it was too late by then. As I got up from the mat that day and looked around the gym, I saw only my brother. He didn't show a hint of a smile; instead, he showed a grimace on his face knowing I was better and should have won. He was disappointed, although he wouldn't say that for several years. He didn't have to. I saw it. No pride built with this achievement, only failure and disappointment.

My wrestling career ended that day. I suited up again the next year and was on the mat for more than half the season. Physically, I was there, but mentally and emotionally, I was done. No matter how hard I tried, no matter how much I accomplished, and no matter how much I dreamed, Dad wasn't coming to any of my matches. If I was going to accomplish anything, it would have to be for me. Accomplishing for me wasn't in my script; it wasn't in my programming. I didn't know how to do that. After trying for so long, all I knew was how to try to prove something to someone else who wasn't there. I needed to build a new foundation of beliefs within me.

I folded my copy of the letter, put it back in the folder and put the folder back in the drawer. I haven't looked at it since. Reading it brought back emotions, but still not the ones I was expecting. I felt more disappointment, frustration and anger than loss. I guess the loss had been there for so long, I had already dealt with that. I didn't lose my father just now; I'd lost him many years ago. What I was losing now was the dream; so losing him, I seemed to be okay with that.

CHAPTER LESSONS

It's too late to reconcile after the other person is gone. I know that seems obvious, yet few of us think of that before it's too late. We always think there'll be another time.

It's never too late to accept someone and cure yourself. Even if the cause of your anger, fear or depression is gone, you can still learn to accept who they were.

Dreams and regrets about the past are part of the programming; rip them up and set real goals to achieve in the future.

Goals are meant for achievement. Set them for yourself, not to impress others. Work toward them with commitment and without fear.

ThoughtShredder Moment

THE FINAL PHASE: REINFORCEMENT

By now you've noticed that you are doing a lot of the same actions over and over again as you read these chapters. You should also be noticing that my life, and likely yours, has some repeating themes in it. I recognized that my father's actions were not what I wanted to repeat and I had a "Bucker moment" on the front lawn with my brother. That one Bucker moment didn't make me a Bucker nor did it create a new life for me. I was still living in the circumstances and seeing the same old actions playing out in new scenes by my father. With each scene, he was reinforcing beliefs and behaviors that I didn't want. With each scene, I had to recognize it, rid myself of it, and replace it with what I wanted to do and be. This is the Final Phase of ThoughtShredder: Reinforcement.

The first time I sat behind the steering wheel of a car, knowing that this wasn't pretend and it was really me who was going to drive, I was scared. I had played the scene over and over in my mind, so I knew what to do. I had read all the assignments from my Driver's Education class, so I knew the rules. Still, it's a different thing when you actually turn the key and step on the gas pedal. The way to get over that fear and to become a licensed driver was to practice and practice and practice. By doing the right things over and over and reinforcing the right behavior, I was able to become a proficient driver.

As you go through the ThoughtShredder process, you will feel doubt and apprehension. This will be reinforced by times when things don't work out perfectly the first time. Stop the doubt right there. Go back to the beginning and reinforce the whole process. It's not a one-time thing; it's an all-the-time thing. I make mistakes often and have to reinforce the process. I also discover new events or circumstances that continue to affect me. I go right back to the process and start again.

ACTION PLAN

Reinforce, Reinforce, Reinforce. Keep doing the process with each new dream you have. Once you start the process with a new dream, you begin turning that dream into a goal. The goal can then be attained.

Make the choice to be a Bucker every day.

SHRED YOUR THOUGHTS HERE

REPLACEMENT THOUGHTS

11

MY BIGGEST FEAR

"What a week!" I thought to myself as I brought my Envoy to a stop inside our garage. It's a three-and-a-half-stall garage that I parked in. We only have two vehicles, but can barely fit them in what originally appeared to us as a cavern that would house ten cars when we first bought the house. As I looked around, I shook my head at all the areas of chaos that can quickly build in my life.

"All this stuff!" I thought. "Do I really need all of this or am I just holding onto useless stuff that feels comfortable to me?" In that same breath, I also wondered where other useless stuff resides. What else am I holding onto that serves me no meaningful or useful purpose?

With little thought to my actions, I clicked the garage door remote and entered the back door to our house. As usual, I hesitated a second to ensure the garage door was closing. On this Friday afternoon, I stood a little longer watching the garage door steadily close, marking the end to a long week. As it tapped the garage floor, a wave of relief came over me knowing the work week was done. Now, I could spend relaxing time with my family. That plan would change after I entered the home of chaos.

Setting my computer bag on the floor, I am quickly pounced on by Carson. He runs to my leg yelling, "Daddy's home!" I pick him up and give him a big hug. Lauren is next, throwing her arms around my waist and giving me a gentle hug. Carson's enthusiasm represents his desire to play with Dad. Lauren is more sensitive and just wants a hug.

I can hear the twins crying in the living room as Tracy feverishly works to complete supper and attempts to keep the calm in our house. Suddenly, I realize that the time management, planning and leadership that I need at the office still can't match what she has to do every day. At least my interactions are with people who completely understand my language. She has to communicate in multiple "languages".

"Where's Megan?" I ask, noting that she hasn't run to me yet.

"I'm in here," she calls from the dining room. "I'm making a picture for you."

My smile shows my appreciation. Suddenly, everything is put into perspective for me. My problems aren't nearly as big as I think they are. I'm surrounded by family I love dearly and everything is going to work out perfectly.

There's an old saying about the weather in Wisconsin: if you don't like it, stick around a little while, it will change. In a house with five children, it's very similar. If you like the way the kids are behaving, stick around a little while. It's bound to change.

Shortly after dinner, the twins go down for their last nap of the day. They haven't napped well so far today, I'm told by Tracy, so this one has to be good if we expect a calm night.

The three older kids are in the dining room coloring and Tracy and I can figure out what movie to watch this evening. Relaxation is interrupted by Lauren.

"Carson!" she cries.

"What's going on?" I ask.

"Carson spilled his juice on my paper." Lauren explains in terror.

I drag myself off my comfortable spot on the couch and think to myself, "I've been up since 4:30 this morning. It sure would be nice to have a quiet night."

"Don't just stand there!" I shout back in utter amazement that three kids can just watch the juice run off the table and onto the carpeting. "Get a towel and clean it up," I finish.

The kids scramble to get the table dried and attempt to soak up what has seeped into the carpet. Disaster one averted and I head back to comfy land.

Before I hit the couch, Megan calls me back. "Lauren's crying."

Reverse pivot, spin around and head back to the dining room. "What's wrong?"

"My picture's ruined!" she cries with tears rolling down her cheeks.

Non-stressed Dad would say, "It's okay honey. I think it looks great. Dad will fix it. It was an accident. Let's work together on another project."

Stressed Dad says, "Really, it's not that big of a deal, just make another one. Carson, what were you thinking? Why do you have that juice in here anyway?" Tonight, I'm stressed Dad and my "words of wisdom" do nothing to relieve the situation. Now Carson is crying too.

"Let's forget about coloring tonight and just watch a movie," I reason, my voice getting slightly louder with each word.

Everyone joins in the living room as the movie starts. Tracy is on the loveseat with Owen sleeping next to her. Aiden is sleeping in the sun room. I'm on the couch alone and the three older kids are on the recliner that really only fits two of them.

Five minutes into the movie, someone starts spinning the recliner around. "Stop that!" a voice shouts. A quiet giggle comes from another voice. "Stop it!"

"Stop spinning the chair! We're trying to watch a movie." I catch my voice mid-sentence and lower it as I see Owen shift his body in discomfort.

What seems like two minutes later, giggles turn into laughs and we can't hear the movie. "Settle down. We can't hear the movie."

"Dad, can you get me some juice?"

"Stop tickling me!"

"Stop spinning the chair."

"I can't see the TV."

"Owen is going to wake up."

"Let's play tag; you're it!"

"We're trying to watch a movie."

"Can we have a snack?"

"Carson pinched me!"

"If I have to say it again, you're all going to bed!"

"What just happened in the movie, I missed it?"

Running ensues. Voices get louder. More juice is needed. Crash!

The sound of glass shattering off the cupboard surface and spreading across the floor silences everything momentarily. That silence is quickly broken by the cries coming from the sun room. Aiden is awake and won't sleep well tonight.

"What happened?" I shout through clenched teeth waiting for the guilty to confess, standing over the accused ready to attack.

"What were you thinking?" I shout over the cries of Aiden. Simultaneously, I grab Carson by the arm, spin him around and raise my hand. I feel the rage inside of me starting to boil to the top. My face turns red while every vein shows in my neck. All of the muscles in my upper body are tight and ready to unleash. To Carson, I must look like some monster rather than his dad.

Like Tiger Woods stopping his swing in mid-backstroke, I stop my arm in mid-action and realize what I am about to do.

Who is this person standing in my body? How did he get here? I've spent twenty years ensuring my temper is in control and now I'm going to let it out on a five-year-old boy who was trying to have fun.

Letting go of Carson's arm, I run down the stairs to the basement and sit in the TV room with my face in my hands. I look at my hands to ensure they are still mine. Who is this guy I've become? Am I becoming Dad?

At all costs, I did not want to be an abuser. I was determined to take a different path. But could I break the programming that was already in me? There were so many occasions it seemed that I could feel my dad buried inside of me waiting to be let out. I stopped him again this time. But could that last? Could I have Dad inside of me waiting to get out? Was I really just like him? I remember being seventeen and finding out just how much like him I really was …

Spending time alone in my own little world feels so comfortable right now. The world of a seventeen-year-old isn't going right. It rarely seems to be. I head up to the attic to spend time alone, wondering why things just don't seem to work out the way I intended. Why doesn't Mom understand me?

The attic in this old house was neatly converted into a bedroom. No one sleeps there anymore now that Mom and I are the only ones living here. It's a quiet room with a small window that doesn't let much light in. It's a good place to sit and think.

A chest on the floor in the corner of the room catches my attention. I've seen it before. It's one of the few things Dad left here. I remember it being full of what I considered junk. My curiosity is up today and I think I'll take another look inside.

I wipe it off and check for spider webs first, then open the latch. Inside is a bunch of old punch cards Dad used to program computers with. I never understood how they worked, but I had seen many of them in the past. There were some old photographs buried under the cards along with some military artifacts: one being an honorable discharge certificate from the Marines. Under that was the most profound find for me: Dad's old Marine uniform.

As I unfolded the crumpled garment of blue and yellow with the yellow fading into the fabric, I could smell the old on it. It was a bit dusty, but really in pretty good condition yet. "I wonder how it would look on me?" I thought fully expecting it to engulf me like the clothes he now wore.

I unfolded the pants, shook them a bit and looked for any moving object. Satisfied that no bugs had gotten into it, I held the pants up to my waistline and judged the length to be possibly a bit short. That's odd, I thought. Dad seemed so tall to me.

I slowly eased one leg into the right pant, then my other leg into the left pant. I pulled them up as high as was comfortable. Yup, just a smidge short, I thought. Then I closed the clasp waiting to see how many other soldiers could fit inside these with me. I was amazed that the clasp, tightened just below my belly button, secured a perfect fit around my waist. Wow, I thought. Dad must have worn these really low and under his belly.

I then tried on the jacket feeling sure that this would reveal the true size my father was … and it did. I unfolded the jacket in the same manner as the pants, making sure nothing was crawling in it. The fabric seemed a little too thick for summer weather. Slipping each arm into the jacket and pulling the shoulders up, I noticed that the shoulders fit as well as the pants. As I buttoned the jacket, it became even more evident that this suit fit me like a glove. It more than fit me; it felt like it was tailored for me. This must have been one of Dad's coats growing up. Nope, that was Dad at twenty-one. You mean he fit into this? Yes. I pulled out a picture from the box of Dad in his uniform. Sure enough, Dad was skinny back then. Not just skinny, but in great shape.

One of those "aha moments" hit me before I knew what an aha moment was. So you're telling me Dad looked just like me when he was my age? Yup.

Part of me asked, what the hell happened to him? How can someone go from where I am now to where he is? He must have made more bad choices than just his ability to be a father. His lifestyle choices went beyond his demeanor with us. It had to be part of his make-up in all areas of his life. He was a Chaos Kid.

The other part of me said, "I know I have a choice to stay this way or follow him." All the while, I thought I had Mom's genes, but it turned out, my body was just like Dad's. He hadn't been predisposed to be 275 pounds from his genetic code. He chose to be that by what he ate, drank and did with his life. I now had the power to choose how I would be by what I ate, drank and did with my life. I had been choosing to buck before this, but now was becoming conscious of the choice.

Still, I was young and the programming hadn't quite kicked in yet. I could have a hundred aha moments like this, but if I didn't know how to get rid of the programming, I still won't change my behavior. I still won't know what the other options are and I will default to Dad.

Sitting in the basement now, thinking back on that day I discovered his uniform, I realize these hands are indeed mine. The actions I took upstairs and those I was about to are also mine. The ability to stop those actions is mine. The intentions are mine; the choices are mine; the actions are mine; and the results will be mine also.

We all get angry. We all overreact at times. The difference for me was that Dad was inside me trying to get out. I felt the rage inside me at times. I saw myself reacting to unleash the rage. I stopped myself just before it escaped, but wondered when Dad would take over in me and I would not be able to contain myself. I needed more Bucker moments.

As I look at my hands, I realize my work on myself isn't done. It likely never will be. The processes I use to erase my blackboard and rip out my programming must continue. This wasn't the first time I wondered if I was becoming Dad. I was guessing it wouldn't be the last time either.

I would get angry at those who reported statistics showing how someone growing up in an alcoholic or abusive family was more likely to become an abuser or an alcoholic. I hated to hear that. I would immediately defend that it was a choice people made, not a curse of birth. If one person, I would reason, can come from that family setting and become successful without alcohol or abuse, then anyone can.

That was a great sentiment that I truly believed with one half of my mind while the other half waited for the Dad in me to show up. In reality, he was already there. It's difficult to go against that programming. If that behavior is what you've seen for twelve or thirteen years, particularly your first twelve or thirteen years of your life, what other options do you know about? My life had so many occasions when I thought I was Dad.

After high school graduation, my vision had always been to go to college. I discussed it with all of my friends and family as if it were a foregone event. But as senior year approached, I had taken no actions toward enrollment other than to look at a few brochures. Once I finally applied in May, I was told there was no more room on campus for the school of my choice. "Irresponsible. Late. You'll never follow through," came Dad's voice inside of me.

I finally enrolled in a community college assuming I would spend just one year there before heading to a *real* college. But finances got in the way and classes got dropped. With a plan of completing eight classes, I ended up with just three classes completed in two semesters. Then I decided it was time to make some money, so I took a year off of college and worked. I started with a factory job, and then broke my wrist. I became a dance instructor, but couldn't sell lessons. I worked in landscaping and bartending, finally settling on working as a stock boy and bagger at a local grocery store.

I was making some money that I could spend and it felt good. Maybe I should just find a job like many other people and forget college? I know college was my goal, but how realistic was that? No one else in my family went to college. Why should I? I felt the familiar pang of quitting deep inside me. I hated quitting. Dad was a quitter. He quit his job, he quit the bar, he quit on us. I'm no quitter. There has to be a way.

One day, I finally pulled out a piece of paper and wrote down "College" on the left side and "Work" on the right side. Then I listed all of what I wanted to do in my life in the middle. Once I was done, I drew a line to the area that I believed could best get me all that I wanted. Most of the lines pointed toward college.

Then I looked at the word "Work" on the paper. I focused on it intently letting all of my emotions out of working without a college degree: all the disdain, fear, disappointment, frustration and sense of failure. Once I was at an emotional peak, I grabbed the paper, ripped it in half and continued to rip the Work side until it there were just tiny shreds left as garbage. Folding up the College side, I put that in my pocket with a sense of pride, determination and will. I knew from that point on that nothing would stop me from attending and graduating college.

ThoughtShredder was born that afternoon. It was likely inside of me, being used subconsciously for some time. Now I had taken it out of my mind and put it into physical action. It felt great and I assumed I was on my way having left Dad behind. After all, he never went to college. I was about to permanently separate myself from his effects. I was going to throw Dad into the darkest dungeon where he would never be heard from again. What a great feeling! But reprogramming doesn't work that way, not that easily. I had done it once, but so many more times were to come.

When I was twenty-five, my fiancée of five years broke up with me. I was alone again, single, without a real job—not one I went to college for—and I asked myself if I was becoming my dad now. Pull out the pad of paper again and start writing and shredding.

When I was let go from my first job out of college, after working there for three years, because of poor choices I made, and then another girlfriend left me, I wondered if I was Dad now. Four months earlier, I was on my way to the executive team. Now my poor choices made me alone, broke, and drinking too much. It sure seemed like Dad.

I would reason with myself, "Well wait, I'm twenty-nine and I still play football and work out. Dad didn't do that at twenty-nine. But I remember him playing softball. Shoot, I haven't escaped him yet."

By age thirty-three I was restarting my career again, this time with a very well-established company, but my latest wife-to-be was out of my life. Alone, but not broke this time, I was partying with my good friend and searching for the newest love. Was I Dad yet? At that point, I considered moving away to get a fresh start and find the girl of my dreams in another area of the country. Part of me wanted to disappear to a new life, but a bigger part of me kept saying, "That's what Dad would do. If you run away, you'll be Dad."

Whenever I gained a few pounds, just two or three—the change didn't have to be much—I wondered if I was now turning into him. When I noticed those pounds, I would think back on all the differences to reassure myself again. Then my workouts picked up again to get rid of those pounds just to make sure. I'm not him yet.

My subconscious was always pulling me back to him, while my conscious mind was trying to convince myself that I wasn't him. Just the fear of that confined me and constrained what I would become.

What was I doing? I was beating myself up and stressing over something that could never happen unless I let it happen.

It was like I imagined one day I would pass through a magical screen and suddenly be him. Thinking about that almost constantly kept me trapped and prevented me from taking chances that could have helped me grow so dramatically in my profession and in my personal life.

Each time I questioned my dad, I would write down what I was feeling. Then I would write down the question, "Am I becoming Dad now?" If I didn't have paper with me, I would visualize writing it in my mind. I could see the paper, see myself writing it down, and see the words clearly on the paper. The will and determination inside of me would well up again. I would feel the power and guidance to overcome this.

With the paper in my hand or the vision in my head, I began to rip the paper. I tore it into shreds and threw it away. Mentally, I was getting rid of the thoughts, emotions and behaviors associated with those childhood memories. I was letting go of them emotionally. The memories were still there, but I was working to get rid of the emotional ties to them and the actions I was so afraid would come out of me because of them.

I knew that if I wanted to get married and have a family of my own someday, I would have to learn new behaviors. I would have to go against the natural programming within me. I would have to learn new actions and reactions. I couldn't just react from instinct. My instinct was wrong based on the lessons from a poor role model.

As I began to dream about a perfect family life I knew the love was there within me, but I was unsure of how I would express it. I didn't want this dream to end like so many others: as just a dream. I didn't want to give up like I did in wrestling. I didn't want poor choices to create failure again. I didn't want to get lucky and find a pot of gold just to blow it in short time. This time I wanted purposeful intent. I wanted to know that the actions I took were going to be in the best interest of my goals. I wanted to know that the old behaviors would be gone. I wanted the fear gone and I wanted Dad out of my life.

Now I face a similar family life as my father did: five children, the first three born about eighteen months from each other and the last two, twins, born three and a half years after the first three. The children are set up as three older ones and two, I am confident, will be known as the "little ones", just like Scott and I were called. But now I realize that I am not my dad. No matter how many similarities I might come up with, I can only be me.

It took many more years to figure out that I wasn't going to turn into my dad. I used to think those years were wasted years. Now I know that as long as I learned something and became a better person, the years were not wasted. Getting rid of Dad was far from a waste of time.

I won't try to fool you into believing I am completely over this. My reprogramming happens almost daily. I have had many minor Bucker moments and other significant ones. What I learned most was that I needed a process to continue erasing my blackboard, bucking the programming my dad put in me, and setting in new programming for who I wanted to be. What I didn't know yet, was about to be revealed in the biggest lesson ever.

CHAPTER LESSONS

There is a Dad inside all of us waiting to get out. It's part of our blackboard or programming.

We are in control of our actions if we consciously make the choice to take control.

We need to follow a process to remove our old programming and wipe off our blackboard.

The process of change is not a one-time event; it is a journey of growth and discovery that lasts our lifetime.

Avoiding being like someone else is still letting that person control you. It means you are not acting for who *you* are and with the great gifts God has given you.

Be the best you for yourself and never give up.

ThoughtShredder Moment

Too often we believe that the past should be buried. Often times we believe the past should be buried with the person whom we have just buried. This is such wrong thinking. Not only is it wrong; it's impossible.

I heard a great man quote the Bible,"A good man leaves an inheritance to his children's children." (Proverbs 13:22).

When I first heard that statement, I immediately thought of money. How much money am I going to leave to my children so I can gauge how good of a father I have been? That's part of it, but a very small part of it. There's a whole lot more.

Every parent leaves an inheritance for his or her children's children. We can't help it. Physically, we pass on similar genes to our children making them short or tall, with black hair or blonde, blue eyes or green. Physically, we are a part of our parents and our children are a part of us.

Our values and beliefs are also passed onto our children. They watch us and learn from our behaviors. They take on the things we want them to take on and those we don't want them to take on. I wonder why my three-year-old says, "Damn it." But I really know he gets it from me whether I intend it or not.

We are a product of our parents to some degree and our children will be a product of us to some degree. Embrace it. I can't pull my dad out of me, but I can work to change the limiting beliefs he gave to me through his actions. I can now build positive beliefs in my children so that I am leaving a positive inheritance for their children's children.

Action Plan

Give this process to your children. Be open and honest with them, letting them know that you are not perfect. Let them know that they can become anyone they want to be and can accomplish anything they want. If they have doubt and fear at any point, work them through ThoughtShredder.

Build an inheritance that will last well beyond the value of money you can give your children.

REPLACEMENT THOUGHTS

12

HEALING THE PAIN

There were so many affects causing the wrong effects in my life, and all of them occurring because I was waiting for the day when I would turn into Dad. I spent most of my childhood in fear of him, then spent much of my adult life fearing I would become him. The impact he had on me was so much greater than I had ever realized before. As I began using ThoughtShredder on the real issues of my life and my past, rather than just on the material things, I began to really grow and heal.

The healing began after I began to understand Dad more. I began to see qualities in him I hadn't seen before. I saw a man I hadn't seen before. He became a different man to me.

How do you love a man who you have described as a monster? How do you love a man who bloodied your nose and whipped your brother? How do you love a man who threatened to kill your mother? How do you love a man who abandoned you, fled to Arizona, and hid there for most of your life?

You do it through one of the greatest qualities God has given to us … forgiveness. First you recognize these beliefs you have of him, and then you shred the ideas that have been stopping you from understanding and forgiving.

When you do this, you will understand his life. You walk a mile, mentally, in his shoes. You understand that life is a growth process and as technology moves higher and higher so too does the human spirit and the ability to recognize and help those with human flaws. You learn that forgiveness is one of the greatest qualities of life. You understand that it is your own ego that calls you into the criticism of him. You understand that by asking why he wasn't more like this person or that person, you are projecting your needs onto him without understanding his needs. You trust that he did the best he could with the information he had available. You believe him when he says his dad was worse. And you live to impart more wisdom in your children than he did to you, just as he imparted more in you than his dad did in him.

Stating all of that seems so easy now. Getting to that realization and bringing it into my heart, that was significantly harder. It took many years of lack of understanding and loss of control. I thought I was in control, but I really wasn't. I thought I knew the track my life was heading down and what was causing it, but I really didn't. I thought I knew how to handle struggles, but I only knew avoidance. I thought I knew what success was and what happiness was, but soon realized that I was looking in the wrong places my whole life. Through one man's lesson, I learned that looking inside of myself was what I was missing. Then the greatest lesson of all came to me through one of the most unlikely sources. And the lessons keep coming.

I began to recall and write my story to help others understand that there are choices we can make as victims to stop being victims. We have the right to choose a different life than the one we were shown and we have the right to choose that at any point in our life. We can be anyone we want to be and accomplish anything we want. We can be the parent, spouse or sibling that we want to be. There are choices. Getting that message to people was my sole intent as I started this writing journey. I quickly learned that my purpose for writing this became a deeper recovery for me and the discovery of a more profound source of guidance. By the end of my writing, my view of recovery became clear. I knew what lesson I was to learn and I embraced it. Now I am sharing it.

My life finally made a turn in a church, but not for the reasons one might think initially. I didn't hear the sermon and suddenly see the light. I didn't sit in a pew alone praying until I heard the Word of God. It wasn't movie-like at all. The lesson came in a simple act involving a man who just wouldn't leave me alone. He started appearing in my life twelve years before I began writing this book.

Through a temp agency, Ronn listed a need for a manager in his distribution company. That need found me looking for work. The temp agency contacted me about a potential management position and that led to my first encounter with Ronn.

Ronn was the controller for a local company that was very successful and continuing to grow, but not very well known to the general public. I met with Ronn a few times for interviews and testing. He struck me as a little odd. He certainly knew his position as controller for this privately held company worth about $20 million in sales annually. It was more his demeanor that struck me as odd.

He explained the position a few different times to me, each time making it sound slightly different. He also noted that someone was currently in the position, but he would be letting that person go so I could take over. That made me uncomfortable, but I needed the job. Two months after our first meeting, I started my finance career again working for Ronn.

The role required that I manage people, which I thoroughly enjoyed. Some of the day-to-day tasks seemed a bit mundane and the systems were antiquated, but I enjoyed the stability and looked forward to learning a new industry.

I quickly learned that my management style and Ronn's clashed. He seemed to believe in the old management style where workers should feel privileged to be working for his company. I believed in developing those reporting to me and providing them opportunities to move up in the company. One of my mentors had taught me that a manager should work hard to promote his employees above himself. That was the true way to move up in a company. Ronn preferred to keep employees in silos. Each employee was to understand the business just enough to do their job better, but not to grow into bigger opportunities.

When Ronn and I met for performance appraisals, he would often hold a stick versus a carrot. He threatened with job loss versus enticing me with a bigger goal. And even though I was the manager, he told me how to evaluate each of my employees and he dictated the wages. Similar to my dad, he seemed better suited to training dogs rather than humans. Instead of using force as Dad did, Ronn used passive threats. He threatened with fear of income loss versus physical pain. Pain in either case was the tool.

With suit and tie as the dress code for men, Ronn went as far as critiquing the ties I chose. My ties were nothing elaborate, but anything outside a solid color or simple stripe was too fancy. In my eyes, Ronn was arrogant and pushy with little to no compassion for the people he hired to work for him. He was the slim version of my dad.

After three years, I couldn't take him any longer. I wrote a scathing resignation letter and left the company for much better surroundings in a company where I would eventually spend ten years working and growing personally and professionally.

I stayed in the same town, which had a population of maybe 100,000 in the greater metro area. It seemed in that small of a town, I would have to run into Ronn at some point, but I was amazed at how often.

Over those next ten years, I "accidentally" ran into Ronn several times a year in the oddest places. I hardly saw the people from his company with whom I made and effort to stay in contact with and yet, Ronn, the guy I wanted to avoid, was showing up seemingly everywhere.

I would see him in bars for happy hour when he was likely twenty years older than me and the crowd I was coming to see. I noticed him at a grocery store on the opposite side of town where I rarely went. Why would I choose that store at that time? Sixty seconds later or earlier and I wouldn't run into him.

My new career provided me the opportunity to travel. I was on several trips to Cleveland with a stop in Detroit and there would be Ronn, in the airport or even on the same plane.

My wife's manager asked me to videotape a charity function for her. She had seen some of the family videos I had put to music and wanted me to do the same for her event. It was around the Fourth of July and her church was putting on a silent auction. During the event, a group of children from the church would be singing patriotic songs as a tribute. I was thrilled to do it as it would be one of my first paid video events.

The first person I saw as I entered the doors of the school where the event was being held was Ronn. At this time, Ronn's kids had to be in college already. What was he doing at an event where six- to ten-year-olds were singing? I didn't know, but I felt like this man was never going to leave me alone. It seemed as though I was now seeing him more than my next-door neighbors. As was customary for me, I acted as if I had not seen him and did my best to avoid coming within eye or earshot of him. And it worked.

During those years, the only words I spoke to him were greetings as I was forced in his path. Beyond that, I avoided any in-depth conversation. That was about to end.

My two daughters were ages seven and five when I finally realized the lesson from Ronn. The two girls had been attending an annual Bible school program for the third year. The program was a week-long event that they attended each day for about three hours, learning about the Bible. The church was across town—closer to my wife's sister's family. Since our older girls were the same age, they could attend the classes together. We thought it would be more enjoyable for all the kids.

At the end of the week, it was customary for the children to put on a show for the parents—performing all the songs they had learned and demonstrating their new knowledge of Jesus and His Works. Each year we had been attending, the event was scheduled for a Friday at noon making it likely that only the parents of the kids would attend. This year was different. Instead of a Friday lunch event, the administration of the church changed the event to Sunday during mass.

We were told on Thursday that the children's show would be conducted during mass on Sunday. This was a church we didn't even belong to and was completely across town where we barely knew any of the members.

Making our decision even easier was the fact that most of the families we did know from that area were going to be out of town. They couldn't make it. Not only did we not belong and not know many people, but the ones we knew weren't going to be there. Our initial decision was not to go. Why go if we don't belong to the church and really don't know anyone? The answer was, because God works in mysterious ways.

After deliberating on it a day or so, guilt got the best of us. If we didn't show, that meant two less kids in the program that they worked so hard to put together. It also meant two more kids wouldn't be able to show their appreciation to the teachers and staff for their hard work. We decided to go to mass at a church across town where we didn't know anyone who would be attending.

Our twins were still in diapers, so getting all five of the kids ready in time to make mass was a challenge, but my wife, with her strong will, dragged me along. We sat in the back of church on a set of chairs against the back wall so we could easily take the twins to the next room if they challenged us.

When the first song of mass started, I heard an unusual sound—unusual for the types of masses I had been at. The sound was from a drum set. I had never heard a drum playing in the traditional churches I had belonged to. The sound caught my attention and I looked over to see if it really was what I had thought. Before I could get my eyes focused on the drums, they stopped at the sight of man playing a guitar. It was Ronn.

"Oh, my God!" I screamed in my head. "What are you doing here? My children have been attending this event for three years now and I have never seen you here. What are the odds that you would be a member here?" I just looked down and shook my head in awe of a man who would not leave me alone.

Aiden brought my attention back to mass as he began to fidget in his car seat. I took that as an opportunity to walk out the door to a waiting area and, hopefully, stay there until mass was over. That way I could just go to the car and avoid Ronn again. As I thought over that plan in my head, something began to change inside of me. I don't know if it was the setting or the mass or the idea that my children were learning about God and I wanted to set an example, or if it was another ThoughtShredder moment, but I began to wonder if I should just say, "Hi," to Ronn and talk to him.

"Why," I thought? "Why not," came the answer. Should I? Shouldn't I? I wasn't really sure, but felt a compulsion to just end this friction. Then I heard the petitions over the speakers that carried the sounds of mass to the outer hall. One was for a lady whose last name was the same as Ronn's. The minister asked that we all pray for her as she continues her battle with cancer. That made up my mind. Could this be Ronn's mother or his wife? What if it was one of his daughters? How terrible would I feel if it was one of mine? I felt a hint of concern, but was mostly a bit nosey. Soon I would be completely concerned.

After mass, I made a point to bring all the kids over to the choir, as Ronn was packing up. He didn't seem to recognize me at first. I thought that was odd; after all, hasn't he been following me around for ten years?

It took a few seconds, but as I extended my hand to him, his face lit up with recognition. I said, "I didn't know your talents extended to playing the guitar." It was an icebreaker and likely the first compliment I had ever given to him.

He laughed lightly then asked how I was. I showed him my family and told him we were doing wonderfully. I explained why were there and that I had never seen him here before. We talked about superficial events for a few more moments, but I could see he was trying to get his guitar equipment packed up. I told him it was nice to see him and we would let him get finished.

My plan was to walk away thinking that I had been the bigger man, arrogance again showing up in me. I had broken the string of avoidance and made the effort to approach him. I had showed him my wonderful family and the success I had become in spite of him. I was satisfied. Whoever was trying to teach me a lesson, obviously was not satisfied.

As I turned to walk away, blanketed in my self-satisfaction, Ronn said, "Are you staying for the picnic?" I knew we didn't want to and I had just proven my point, so why would I stay longer? But Ronn continued before I could answer, "I'll be done in a minute. I'll see you outside." He seemed sincere as though he honestly wanted to talk to me.

We hung around the outer hall meeting the minister and his family, some church members from my sister-in-law's neighborhood and some parents of the other children. Finally, Ronn came out and found me. He had now sought me out. We discussed where we were in our careers now and talked a little more about our families. Then I asked him if he was related to the lady who was mentioned in church.

Ronn's face took on human form. I know that sounds so cruel, but all this time I had seen him as another image of my dad— a cruel man who didn't have a clue about how to treat other people. He seemed like an emotionless machine to me with profit as his only goal. Now I saw emotion. I'm certain it was always there, but I blinded myself to seeing it in him for all the years I had known him and replaced him for Dad.

He nodded and said, "She's my wife." I began to understand the lesson for me. In that moment, I believe God stopped time for me. He allowed me to stand there, close my eyes and drift up to him so he could hand the lesson to me personally. I came back to that moment forever changed. This was a *person* standing in front of me. He had always been a person. I had been the one to put the image of him in my head. I had carried that image with me for so long. It was my choice. I had never given him the chance to prove his human qualities. And, in all honesty, no one should have to prove it. I should know they exist. This moment was about my faults.

Ronn continued to explain the fight his wife was undertaking and relayed that this was her second diagnosis. She had cancer some ten years earlier, was cured, and now it came back. Through her struggle with treatment, she was also helping to manage the wedding plans of their daughter. What a difficult time this must be. Ronn looked strong in faith perspective. He seemed full of faith and compassion, but a toll was being taken on him physically. He was full of hope, but spent on energy. Surely, this was not the man I knew ten years ago. There's no way this much compassion and care can come from Ronn. Sure it can, had I allowed him to show it to me and had I allowed myself to see it.

God appears to us in the most unusual ways. All this time since I left that company, as Ronn was appearing to me, he had a lesson for me. I wasn't ready to see it or hear it. Finally, on this day I was ready, and he delivered.

Buddha wrote, "When the student is ready, the teacher will appear." I am a firm believer in that. Ronn was my teacher and he was appearing to me over and over, but I was not ready to listen or to learn before. For some reason on this day I was ready and was rewarded with the greatest lesson of my life.

The lesson he gave me was forgiveness. At the moment, it was as if I visited God in that church hallway. I suddenly felt a sense of endless forgiveness. I forgave Ronn for all that I had presumed he was. It was not the type of forgiveness that we are accustomed to. It was not the kind where one apologizes to us, we state we forgive them, and tell them to go forth and do no wrong like that again. It was not like that at all. Ronn had nothing to apologize for. He was just being the Ronn that God created. I was projecting my father onto him as I had with so many authority figures before and since. I was wrong. I forgave him by apologizing to God and forgiving myself. I made a mistake; I was wrong; I am sorry; and I forgive myself. Now I will go forth trying not to act like that again.

The rain began to fall outside the church, so we packed our kids up and I ran to get the van. I backed it up to the front doors and we loaded the kids in. Just as I put the van in drive, a knock came to my window. It was Ronn. He told me it was good to see me again and wished me luck. I looked into his eyes as the rain fell on him and wondered if he knew why he was there for me. I got to see God twice that day. What a treat.

When we got home, I let Tracy deal with the twins. I went to my journal and wrote down all of the characteristics I had thought were a part of Ronn. I put all of the past emotion and bitterness toward him on that paper. When I was finished, I ripped it up and threw it away. Then I wrote all of the new qualities I had seen in him: the compassion, the intelligent resolve, the faith, the integrity, and the selflessness. All of these combined into the new image I had of Ronn, now that the old was ripped away.

I felt relieved and at peace. How ironic. I became relieved once I changed my image of Ronn. He didn't change; I did. I could have easily kept the bitterness and self-serving image I had of Ronn. I could have continued to complain about him at every opportunity when someone brought up a bad leader. I could have continued to demand that he change to appease me. Instead, by looking inside of me and changing me, I got the reward of peace. Another Bucker moment had been shown to me.

Replacement Thoughts

13

FORGIVING MY DAD

As I lay in bed that night, feeling so good about the change in me, another revelation hit. "Oh, my God!" I said out loud and jumped from my bed. Tracy twisted in bed for a second, but quickly was back to sleep. I headed down the steps, all the way to the basement. I pulled out my journal again and wrote down these five words:

"Dad was a person too."

That seems so obvious now, but became a revelation to me then. My practice of writing and ripping up memories and old beliefs had helped me to uncover my predispositions. It was getting to the root memories that were driving my actions. Even if I logically didn't believe those concepts anymore, the memories and emotions attached to them seemed to be driving my actions. I was reacting based on an old, outdated belief system that had been built as the foundation of my life. It was the program set up in images of my past. It wasn't the words used or the actual events. It was the emotion I tied to them. It was the reasoning I put as images for those doing these acts.

I had always assumed that everyone knew what I wanted and needed. I assumed they had a blackboard full of all my needs. Instead of providing me with these needs, they intentionally acted against them. People who looked like or acted like my dad knew what I wanted and made sure I didn't get it. Just like I assumed Dad did. He knew what I wanted and needed and was intentionally holding it back from me. How crazy of a thought is that?

Dad wasn't the image that I had created. He was a man who made mistakes like we all do. A man who did what he did based on what he knew at the time. I began to feel sorry for him, sorry that he didn't have a mentor to teach him. I felt sorry that for him, as teachers appeared, he never seemed ready. He lacked the understanding of who he could be.

I began to wonder about his life and how he was taught to act. During a conversation with my grandmother, she had told me that Dad would go to his father's grave at night, crying and asking him for answers. I was waiting for answers from Dad, while he was waiting for the same answers from his dad. As I waited for my dad to show up at the events I was in and show his pride, my dad was waiting for his father to show his pride.

I can imagine my dad now, sitting at that gravesite asking his father the same questions I asked of my dad. "Dad, didn't you know that loving me meant providing for me at all times? It meant supporting me? It meant being there when I had my proudest moments even if the accomplishments were far less than you expected? Didn't you know that dying meant abandonment and you left me wondering whom I would turn to for advice and support? Didn't you know that a father's love is unconditional? Didn't you remember your father's love?"

I can imagine Dad at that gravesite now. I imagine that he asked why. Why did you leave me at age seven? What did I do to cause your heart attack? Why did I not seem good enough for you?

In those moments, I realized it was not only Ronn who I was forgiving, it was also my dad. I forgave my dad for acting the way he did and I gave myself permission to feel what he must have felt his whole life—lost, confused, alone, and trodden on.

It began to make sense that he lacked the understanding of how to act another way. He missed a part of his life and a part of love that should have been his father. His father left him when he was just a child. I believe somewhere in Dad's subconscious mind, Dad was ensuring that he too fulfilled that "prophecy". He was behaving in ways to ensure that his children lost their father too. His programming kicked in. He made decisions based on this even though he didn't know it or likely want it. My dad was getting not what he wanted from life, but what he expected. He only knew loss and was unwittingly ensuring that loss is exactly what he got.

As I thought about all of these new ideas about Dad, all the forgiveness in the world seemed to come to me. I recalled what Mark Twain stated about forgiveness. He said, "Forgiveness is the fragrance the violet sheds on the heel that has crushed it." I remembered hearing that just before my meeting with Ronn and now I was putting it all together. That phrase took on an exponential meaning to me. I felt as though Dad had been "crushing" me under his heel all through my childhood. Now was my time to release the fragrance of forgiveness. The fragrance I needed to release was my ability and desire to help others understand.

Ronn was brought to me to teach me something. I was now ready and accepting the lesson. To forgive Dad like the violet does, I thought it would be incredibly difficult given the events of my life. Surprisingly, it wasn't difficult at all. It was simply a letting go and letting God take over.

In my act of forgiveness for Ronn, Ronn became the person he always was: the person he wanted to be, not the image I had created. The absence of that grudge was like cutting the rope on an anchor. It gave me freedom and understanding—a clearer mind so that I could forgive Dad.

As I forgave Dad, he became the person he wanted to be, not the image I had created. In those moments, I realized that I could never become him nor could I become the image I had created of him. Who I could become was anyone I wanted to be. If I created the image, I could become that person. I no longer had to be held back by the limitations of my thoughts of Dad. For the first time since I stepped onto the sidewalk outside my college dorm my freshman year, I felt I had the whole world open to me. I could choose to do or be anything I wanted. Now I look forward with great anticipation to the rest of my life becoming whomever I want. Now I can help others to be anyone they want.

The way to forgive, to make a fresh start, to become divinely inspired, is to forgive divinely. It means to open yourself up to your own faults. It means to accept yourself and others for who they are. It means understanding them and understanding yourself. It's connecting with a divine power whether you believe that to be God, Buddha, Krishna, the sun, the moon, the universe; whatever that means to you, become one with it. Understand we are all connected. We all have paths taken and paths yet to be followed. Those past paths have dug patterns into our brains that drive us to act in certain ways. We need a process to recognize those patterns, rid ourselves of them, and replace them with what we really want.

Forgiveness removes the armor that has protected us for so many years. Unfortunately, it has protected us from living the ultimate dream of peace and happiness. It's like opening the window on the first day of spring. You wake to bright sunshine reflecting off the mirror in your bedroom. The steps leading you downstairs to the kitchen have a glow as the rays are filtered through the panels in the front door. You walk to the kitchen for that first cup of coffee and are temporarily blinded by rays bouncing off your stove. Out the window you can see just a hint of green speckled within the brown grass; life is starting over. A robin swoops by as you open the window a crack and immediately the cool air hits you and you breathe in that wonderful fragrance of spring. That's how forgiveness feels. The anger, the grudge that you have been carrying with you, is an anchor pulling you down and away from your dreams. Forgiveness dissipates the anchor into dust and the fresh spring air sweeps it out the window as that same crisp air captures it and sends it into the atmosphere, away from you forever. Let go of it.

Forgiveness wasn't an act of walking up to the person and stating, "I forgive you;" meaning, "You have done wrong and now I am okay with it. Don't do it again." That's how I teach my children to apologize. "Say you're sorry, show remorse, now the other one forgives you and you hug."

That's someone saying, "I was wrong. I hurt you and I am sorry. I won't do it again."

The other person in return is saying, "You're right, you were wrong. It's okay, but don't do it again."

That type of forgiveness is a learning forgiveness. You did wrong; you acted poorly and inappropriately and are now learning a better way to act. If that situation comes up again, you'll know one way not to react. That is a great way to learn, to grow, and become a better person. That's one way to forgive, but it's not *the* way. I learned *the* way and have been liberated ever since.

Without forgiveness and ThoughtShredder you will let the thoughts and comments from others control you. You will never live the life you were intended here to live. You will exist within the confines of their set parameters, never to stretch to the limitless power of you, never to become a Bucker.

Take control now and become a Bucker.

REPLACEMENT THOUGHTS

14

THE PROCESS

Countless research has been done noting the affects of childhood on who we become as adults. In one piece by Larry Bilotta entitled, "It Only Takes One to Heal a Marriage," Bilotta notes that we all grow up on a spectrum between *chaos* and *always*. On one end of the spectrum is the chaos childhood filled with things like abandonment, abuse, alcohol, drugs, and potentially death. On the other end of the spectrum is the always childhood where parents were firm but fair, treated each child as a unique being, and celebrated the unique successes of the children.

For many who don't understand their choices, adult life follows directly from childhood experiences. We grow up living a life pretty similar to that of our parents and we take on many of the habits our parents or guardians had. It makes sense. We watch these habits play out in our parents and are taught the values handed down by them.

These experiences as a child create what I call the blackboard of our lives. Our influences are etched into the blackboard and continue to build upon each other. These are the set of circumstances, events and relationships that form who we are as adults. The blackboard begins to form the basis of who we are. It will control us in our adult lives.

As I mentioned in my story earlier, I refer to this as a blackboard because, like a teacher's blackboard, we often assume that what is written there is accepted as accurate, true, and fact. It is not up for debate. We don't even realize this is happening. It reminds me of the concept of electricity. I don't know how it works or why it works, but I use it every day. I take it for granted each day when I flip on the light switch that electricity is powering my ability to eliminate the darkness. How and why this blackboard runs my life is not important. That it does is very important.

The Bucker understands the concept of the blackboard. Others call it programming, nature, upbringing, or hard-wiring. Certainly some of our adult events help shape us also, but the foundational elements that are buried deep in our brains are the things that drive us most. They set up the foundation of beliefs and values that we allow to run our lives. We carry that blackboard with us our entire lives.

I'm not a qualified analyst on childhood behavior, so I won't pretend to know more than that. The important concept is that we all are driven in part by the events of our past.

For some, the blackboard is perfectly written on. Their childhood experiences were with parents who were firm, but fair, treated them as unique individuals and celebrated successes. Some grew up in a loving, nurturing family without abuse or neglect. Many of us grew up in homes full of chaos and appear destined to live chaotic adult lives as well.

Many of us, without realizing it, believe we cannot change it. This is when you hear phrases like, "That's the way I was raised," or "I got that from my dad." True statements; but unfortunately, they are too often followed by, "I can't help it." That's where they are wrong.

A Bucker is a person who defies his upbringing, his childhood teachings, and decides he or she wants a different life: a different set of beliefs that will create different behaviors and different results from his or her childhood teachings. In general, a Bucker is someone who is farther on the chaos end of the spectrum having grown up in a family of chaos. If you read my story, you know that I grew up in a chaos household primarily because of an abusive, alcoholic father.

I want to be very clear on one point. Even though I grew up in a chaos house, doesn't mean you had to in order to use the ThoughtShredder process. This can be used on any limiting belief that you know you have or are not yet aware that you have. As you go through the process, you'll discover beliefs and sources of those beliefs that have been hidden to you by your own mind. Trust me on that.

As the events of my childhood were occurring, I slowly and naturally began a process to clear parts of my blackboard. As I continued the process I began to discover more limiting beliefs buried deep within me. There were the incidents with Dad, those were easy to find; I had buried them pretty deep, but they were easy to uncover. There were also subtle moments, seemingly insignificant moments, that were having a dramatic affect on me. These were statements from best friends, reactions from coaches, and opinions of teammates. These were the little things that we hear daily and just brush off ... or do we? When you've been in an abusive relationship, it's easy to cling to the next person who provides hope for you. When you are a seven-year-old child making a conscious decision to buck your father, you become vulnerable to the programming of others. As I set out on this unknown journey to create my own programming, I left space on my blackboard clear for anyone to write on. I didn't know I was doing it ... I was seven.

The danger I found in becoming a Bucker without another true role model to provide guidance is that the mind will take on any and all advice. This can happen to the point of believing in contradictory things or worse, not really knowing what you believe in. There are advantages too. With a clean slate, I was willing to try many things in order to define what I would believe in and I was willing to fail many times too.

The method I used to erase parts of my blackboard is called ThoughtShredder. It is an incredibly simple process with four steps I call the Four R's. They are as basic to changing your life as the three R's are to education: Reading, wRiting and aRithmatic. These Four R's are: *Recognize, Rid, Replace,* and *Reinforce.*

I learned through my journey that all four steps are critical. Recognize means to remember the events and beliefs that are hindering you. Rid means to rip them up, erase them from your blackboard and stop them from controlling you. Replace is the process of creating new beliefs and new habits that are purposeful. Reinforce means you will have to do this over and over to ensure the habit sticks and to eliminate other bad habits you haven't thought of yet.

This whole process is nothing new. Any life coach or performance coach will tell you that visualization, affirmations, and intentions are all necessary to become the person you want to be, and to reach the success you want to reach. This is The Replacement Phase and it works wonderfully ... unless you have a blackboard filled with events from a chaos childhood.

This chaos childhood creates a belief structure that is buried deep within us. It is etched into our blackboard rather than just written there with erasable chalk. I have found during periods of my life that visualization alone did not work. Affirmations and intentions listed on a piece of paper alone did not work. The beliefs I had buried deep within me would not allow the intentions to take full hold. Let me explain with an example.

Imagine a concrete driveway. When it is first built it requires several layers. First there is the base ground that is leveled as much as possible. A layer of stones or crushed rock is raked over the top of the ground. This is covered with sand that is compressed through a stamping process. Finally, the concrete is poured over the top of the sand in sections. Each section is separated by a rubber lining to allow expansion. Now you have wonderful driveway that serves a great purpose for your home.

What happens fifteen to twenty years later, especially in Wisconsin with the harsh winters? That driveway that has served a wonderful purpose for so many years is now chipping, cracking, and heaving. Now, it is getting old and beat up. Cracks are forming; things are growing from between the cracks, and sections are shifting and rising to make it uneven. It had a purpose at one time, and it fulfilled that purpose very well (just like some of those old thoughts of yours).

Now you want to replace it with a brick driveway that will serve an even better purpose since it will be more durable and aesthetically pleasing. You have a vision of this new driveway. It is made of brick pavers placed in a lattice pattern. The red brick is accented with white stone forming edges on both sides. The vision you have for this is clear, just like many of your other goals. But the vision won't get the driveway done. Wanting it, visualizing it, and affirming it isn't enough; you have to act. The action is not just in the effort to create the new driveway. There has to be something done with the current driveway.

How do you build your new driveway? What are the first steps? Well, I'll bet you wouldn't just throw sand or ground over the old driveway and lay the new bricks on top, would you? That seems like the easy way and might work in the short term. You've leveled the area and put the bricks smoothly and evenly on top, but what happens in a short time? The old foundation continues to crack and heave. Pretty soon the old driveway is breaking the new driveway apart. Can you imagine how unstable and messy that would be? I wonder how unstable some of our new thoughts are if we haven't taken care of the old foundational thoughts we have.

Instead, the first act you would likely take in order to build that new driveway you have visualized is to get the biggest sledgehammer you could find and start whacking away at the old foundation. You would smash the old stuff, rip it out, and throw it in the dumpster, never to be seen again.

Once the old foundation is torn out, you can build a fresh new driveway in the same place. Now the bricklaying is much easier, and the driveway is much more attractive. It serves the new purpose you intended without the underlying mess. The new foundation is stable again.

There is a similar process we have to go through in order to really become the person we want to be. We can't just want something. We can't just wish for something. We can't just set a vision to have something or achieve something. We can't just set affirmations or intentions. Having the vision and setting affirmations and intentions are good, but first we need to get rid of the old mental foundation that was laid during our childhood and continues to be reinforced. We have to recognize the old foundation, rip it up, and rid ourselves of it, and then replace it with a new foundation of thoughts that create the new us with new actions and new results.

This is exactly how the ThoughtShredder works. Many of your old thoughts served a purpose for you at one time, but no longer serve you now. You have grown to know that you have more to accomplish and have more ability than before. Just like the old driveway, had it continued to be used, would have slowly worn down the vehicles that drove on it; your old, destructive thoughts are wearing you down. They are stopping you from becoming who you really want to be. Take a parenthetical sledgehammer to those thoughts, rip them out, throw them away, and build new layers of thought on who you really can be.

PHASE ONE: RECOGNIZE

This is so easy, so basic a step. That might be exactly what you are thinking now. It is easy to a point, but the real work is in this phase. It's easy to find some of these concepts, ideas, or beliefs that have been limiting you. Most of us can think back to times in our youth or young adult life when negative events affected us. These are what many refer to as the "low hanging fruit". It's easy to find these and pluck them from the tree. It takes effort to find the rest of the gems.

Start with these easy concepts. Think back to an event that caused a limit in you, perhaps something that happened recently if that is easier. If you know of an event in your childhood, use that one. Use the first one that hits you. If you are still struggling, think of an action you would like to take, but have always thought of yourself as not having the ability, knowledge, or courage to accomplish. Once you have that action, think back to why you doubt yourself. What is it that tells me I can't do this? The answer to that will be your first R: *Recognition*.

An example for me goes all the way back to seventh grade, twenty-eight years ago. In the small school we attended, there was no seventh or eighth grade football program; we had to wait until high school. My best friend at the time, Matt, and I loved to play football. I loved playing many sports. I was wrestling when I was in kindergarten, shooting hoops from the day I could dribble a ball, throwing a Frisbee, putting bat on ball, whatever sport was available: I loved being part of it. Matt was slightly less inclined and, because of that, I seemed to be just a little better than him at most sports. Matt didn't care. He seemed to recognize that was just the way it was. He was more interested in working after school while I was interested in playing.

Matt had an idea for us as our seventh grade year began. He suggested that he and I join the seventh grade cross-country team to start getting in shape for football in two years. I thought it was a great idea so we signed up. Until that point in my life, I had not run further than the extent of my driveway to catch the school bus—some 200 yards perhaps. Now I was expected to run miles. That didn't work very well from the start.

Matt, on the other hand, picked it up very well. Even though his legs were thicker than mine and seemed destined to carry him into a linebacker position, he was a more natural distance runner than I. Here was the first sport that Matt was decidedly better at than I.

One day towards the end of a practice run, Matt was waiting for me at the finish line. I crossed the line in pure exhaustion, placed one hand on my hip and the other on Matt's shoulder, bracing myself on him. After a few minutes, I collected myself and we walked back to the locker room together. As we walked, Matt said something to me that I have not only remembered for all these years, but I have since built on it with more and more evidence to ensure it is true. Matt told me with a bit of a laugh in his voice, as if to attempt to lessen the sting, "You might be good at a lot of sports, but you stink at distance running." My competitive, likely arrogant, nature came out immediately and I defended myself stating that running wasn't really much of a sport. After all, there's no one on the other side trying to stop you.

Deep down that hurt. Here was my best friend telling me for the first time that I wasn't good at something. He might have previously thought it about other things, but he never stated it to me like he did this time. Imagine a thirteen-year-old, impressionable kid just starting to like girls, trying to find his identity, now being told he stinks at something. This wasn't a teacher or coach or cousin or other acquaintance stating this. That I could brush off with a, "What do you know?" comment. This was the person I thought knew me best. If he thinks it, it must be true.

I didn't run distance again until I was twenty-seven years old. Even then, I got up to three miles and quit. That wasn't me. I'm not a distance runner. I believed that so much that I made sure I never ran more that 200 yards again for fourteen years. I told everyone who asked that I was a sprinter by design and by desire. Though for years of high school track, I ran the 100-meter and 200-meter dashes, along with competing in pole-vault, I wasn't going any further because I "stunk" at it.

Matt didn't mean any harm with his comments. He was merely telling me about an observation he made based on what he knew about me. The results were right in front of us and he was just stating his opinion of the evidence. He was unwittingly, without malice sending out a negative thought and I took hold of it, accepted it, set it in the base of my brain, and built all the necessary conditions to ensure it was true.

That's not me anymore. As I write this, I am utilizing the Thought-Shredder process to create the distance runner in me. Not only am I a distance runner who can now compete in 5K and 10K events, but I completed my first half marathon. Those old, negative thoughts started by a dear friend when I was impressionable had a lot of junk built on top of them.

I didn't complete this change by just visualizing it. I had been trying that for years. I first had to go back in my memory and find that moment where my belief about me was created. I had to find the foundation. Once I did, I could follow the rest of the process to build the new me in this area of my life. In order to awaken the Bucker in you, you have to determine what the programming is that needs changing.

One of the hardest parts of this phase is that it causes us to challenge some of those long-held beliefs we hold dear to us. We remember the statement or the foundation of the belief, but have difficulty in challenging ourselves to think differently. If you are a natural Bucker, it's much easier. We want to defy our programming instantly. If you are not used to being a Bucker, it takes effort to suspend the doubt and believe that these thoughts are limiting.

This is also a phase where many emotions can be discovered. You will likely feel tension in yourself as you recall some of these events. When you feel tension or uneasiness in your stomach you know you're on the right path. Keep digging. It's easy to give up at this point, don't. Keep digging until you have the issue at hand. Then write the belief down. Next to that belief, write down the emotion you felt as you relived the events. This will become important.

Start slowly. Take the low-hanging fruit. Make a habit of questioning those old beliefs and begin the rest of the process.

Phase Two: Rid

Many of the people I meet have paper shredders. Many offices that I go into have similar devices. These shredders are meant to shred documents, credit cards, etc. that might reveal to others something personal about you or your business. Part of the desire for this is due to our egos wanting privacy, not letting others know who we really are. Another part of this is to avoid real hazards that take the form of unscrupulous individuals harming us through financial gain for themselves. This latter part is a real risk that should be mitigated. However, I would submit to you that most, if not all, of us do much more damage to ourselves with the negative thoughts we have than anyone could do with the documents they would find from us.

Negative thoughts and the bad habits formed from those negative thoughts prevent us from reaching our potential. They drag us down and stop us from pursuing the purpose we have intended for ourselves. They block us from acting on the intuitive thoughts of genius that are within us all. Instead of acting on an impulse or an idea that we instantly receive and know is going to direct us right down the path of our intent, we let negative thoughts convince us that we can't do it. We need to rid ourselves of these thoughts.

Charles Haanel, the great writer and entrepreneur of the late 19th century wrote in his book, *The Master Key System*, the same information I am giving you now. He knew it in 1890 as did all the great inventors of our time. In Mr. Haanel's words:

"… if we have stored away nothing but courageous thought, if we have been optimistic, positive, and have immediately thrown any negative thought on the scrap pile, have refused to have anything to do with it, have refused to associate with it or become identified with it in any way; what then is the result? Our mental material is now of the best kind …"

He goes on to write about the mental cleaning that must take place in our minds:

"The thing to do is to have a mental housecleaning and to have this housecleaning every day, and keep the house clean. When this mental housecleaning process has been completed, the material that is left will be suitable for the making of the kind of ideals or mental images which we desire to realize."

You will be doing this with Phase Two. Take those thoughts, events and beliefs that you recognize and shred them. Pull out a tablet or pad of paper. Write them down. Take hold of that page firmly and tear it out. Tear it with passion. Remove it completely from that tablet. I know, your grade school teacher told you never to tear the pages, but that is a limiting thought. I give you permission to tear out those pages.

Now, as you hold the page in your hands, take one more look at the bad habit or negative thought and let it sink into your mind and heart. Read it aloud to hear how silly and limiting it is. Now put it in that paper shredder and hit the button. Listen to it shred. As you hear that, imagine that same thought being removed and shredded from your mind. It no longer exists there.

If you don't have a paper shredder handy, with both hands, rip that page into the tiniest pieces possible. Rip it with dramatic motions. Take all of those pieces and throw them into your fireplace, bag them up and shove them deep into the bottom of your garbage, or squash them in your trash compactor.

That is all they are good for, trash. They serve no purpose in your life or in your mind. Tear them out of your mind and shred them forever. Shred the thoughts that created destruction. Now you have cleared the area; you've erased part of the blackboard. Now you are ready to replace.

PHASE THREE: REPLACE

Now that your "brain closet" is clear of that thought, it can be filled with the new vision of who you can be. Now start to visualize how great you are and how easy it is to achieve your goals. Create the vision of who you want to be with passion.

You may be thinking, "But I can't visualize who I want to be." If that is your problem, you have two choices: one, continue to shred the thoughts that make that up, or two, find an imagination mentor.

The imagination mentor is someone who can readily visualize using their imagination to create wonderful dreams. For me, my five children have wonderful imaginations. I imagine that I once possessed that quality also, but life diminished it. I now watch them create wonderful imaginative objects.

My six-year-old loves to play hockey in the house. He has several toy sticks, but doesn't own a puck. Do you think that stops him? No way. He finds a ball, a sock, anything not valuable and pretends it's a puck. Ice? The whole house is his rink.

Don't get too complicated. Be simple about your imagination. Don't hold back. If a living room can be a hockey rink in his mind, then a treadmill can be the Boston Marathon for me. Find your imaginative ability and leverage it: build it and use it.

Once you've done this, the actions you need to take to get to those goals will come to you. You'll see them in real life. You'll recognize them and take advantage of them. You'll believe you can do it, and then you'll see the way.

Don't stop with one act. Begin to reinforce the process immediately.

PHASE FOUR: REINFORCE

What we learn is not nearly as important as what we re-learn. Reinforcement is the process of building deeper in our minds the concepts and beliefs we truly want. Knowledge is great; however, if I learn something today and forget it tomorrow, what good was it?

That too often happens in people's lives. They learn a great technique in a seminar and completely forget it by the time they get back home. You have a desire to change, but you've held onto those old beliefs for a long time. Most of your life's actions have been a part of those beliefs. Your old thoughts will creep back into your mind because of a picture you see, an accomplishment or failure you are reminded of, or even a comment someone makes to you. These are powerful reinforcements of the old way. You need to break them down with powerful reinforcement of the new way.

The analogy of the driveway is important here. When the new driveway is built, it is reinforced with a new foundation. Metal bars might be put into the concrete or concrete is put between the bricks to build more strength. For buildings, driveways and other inanimate things, reinforcement is done once. Then we move onto the next project.

We are humans. We are constantly growing and changing. We have many different experiences with new concepts, new ideas and new actions to learn that create habits. Our reinforcement can't be a one-time event. We have to continue to build on the replacement beliefs and actions to ensure they become habits.

I have often found that I learn even more when I teach. This is part of reinforcement: do it again and again and again. When you are done with that, teach someone else so you have to do it again. Continue to reinforce until you don't even realize you are doing it anymore. It is then called a habit.

The great benefit of reinforcement for me was that it allowed me to dig deeper and deeper into parts of my past I had forgotten about. My conscious mind forgot, but my subconscious was continuing to drive my habits.

To become a Bucker you have to follow a process. You have to first identify what behavior you want to change before you can begin any ThoughtShredder steps. Once you've determined the change you want in you, then begin to recognize the deep-seated beliefs you have that are controlling those actions. Once you have them, begin to rid yourself of them; this cleans the "mental closet". With a clean foundation, you can now build new images of yourself, replacing the old images. Replacing the old images will begin to replace the old actions. As new actions are taken, new results will follow. It's time to reinforce your new actions.

As you follow this process, you will begin to uncover thoughts you didn't know existed. Just like digging up that old driveway, you might find another foundation under the original that you didn't know existed and it is the root of the problem. As I followed the process, I began to have dreams during my sleep about events in my life that I thought I had totally forgotten or dismissed. Trust me, you never truly forget; you just have difficulty bringing those memories to your current, conscious mind. They're there and likely hindering you without you even realizing it.

My dreams were about statements my dad had made to me and memories of events that were now being played back like a high definition DVD. The videos were playing back my failures: losing wrestling matches or important football games, giving up when I was about to be beat rather than committing to the very end, and not even trying to begin with because of a fear of failure.

By reinforcing the first three steps, I was able to uncover more and more memories that were buried deep inside my brain. I was able to let many of these go and discover more. The process became liberating. But true liberation didn't come until I found one belief that permeated all others. Once I found this, I also discovered the one act that is the only act to final recovery.

Recall what you read in Chapter 12: that this process can be easy for the low-hanging fruit. Those of us who grew up in abusive relationships have memories and beliefs etched in the blackboard. They often feel burned into them and if we touch them, we will get burned again. This is where the process becomes so liberating. This is also where the effort in the process has to build. Deep issues need deep commitment to the process. There is likely a fear in you to return to those memories again. Start the process right there. Recognize that fear, rid yourself of it, replace it with what you know to be true and right, then reinforce it with courage. Once you start the process there, you'll be able to tackle those deeper issues.

Keep going. Make ThoughtShredder a part of every day for yourself. Let people see you ripping up pages and tearing out the old beliefs. Then let them see you succeed with your new thoughts and new accomplishments.

I am always interested in the stories of others. Share your thoughts and experiences as a Bucker with me. Together we can help so many find and let out the Bucker in them.

REPLACEMENT THOUGHTS

About The Author

Chris Elliott is a practicing Servant Leader with more than twenty years of experience helping organizations implement change through process, technology and structure, including Schneider National, Integrys Energy Group and PolyOne. He is certified in Change Acceleration Process and relies heavily on ADKAR methodology to implement change. His journey through Servant Leadership has helped him create processes that allow individuals to get in touch with their past in order to create the future each wants. His unique ThoughtShredder techniques help individuals, teams and organizations understand the values and beliefs that drive them and provide steps to change what is keeping us all from reaching our goals. Chris and his wife Tracy have five children ranging in age from four to eleven, all of whom continue to teach Chris improved communication.